THE TRAGEDY OF

King Richard the Second

E D I T E D   B Y

George Lyman Kittredge

Revised by Irving Ribner

THE TRAGEDY OF

William Shakespeare

King Richard
the Second

XEROX COLLEGE PUBLISHING

LEXINGTON, MASSACHUSETTS • TORONTO

Though this be all, do not so quickly go.
I shall remember more. Bid him — ah, what? —   65
With all good speed at Plashy visit me.
Alack, and what shall good old York there see
But empty lodgings and unfurnish'd walls,
Unpeopled offices, untrodden stones?
And what hear there for welcome but my groans?   70
Therefore commend me — let him not come there
To seek out sorrow that dwells everywhere.
Desolate, desolate will I hence and die!
The last leave of thee takes my weeping eye.   *Exeunt.*

◇◇◇◇◇◇◇◇◇◇◇◇◇◇◇◇

SCENE III. [*The lists at Coventry.*]

Enter Lord Marshal *and the* Duke Aumerle.

MAR.   My Lord Aumerle, is Harry Hereford arm'd?

AUM.   Yea, at all points, and longs to enter in.

MAR.   The Duke of Norfolk, sprightfully and bold,
Stays but the summons of the appellant's trumpet.

AUM.   Why, then the champions are prepar'd, and stay   5
For nothing but his Majesty's approach.

The trumpets sound and the King
enters with his Nobles, Gaunt, Bushy,
Bagot, Green, *and others. When they
are set, enter* Mowbray the Duke
of Norfolk *in arms, defendant, and*
Herald.

furnish'd stripped of the arras (tapestry hangings) with which the walls of the
apartments would be covered when the castle was occupied [K]. 69 *Unpeopled
offices* empty places where domestic work was performed, the servants all de-
parted.
    I.III. 1 *Lord Aumerle* serving as High Constable of England and thus, with the
Lord Marshal, responsible for the conduct of the combat.   2 *in* into the lists.
3 *sprightfully* with spirit. *bold* boldly.   4 *appellant's* accuser's.

KING.   Marshal, demand of yonder champion
        The cause of his arrival here in arms.
        Ask him his name and orderly proceed
        To swear him in the justice of his cause.   10

MAR.   In God's name and the King's, say who thou art,
        And why thou comest thus knightly clad in arms;
        Against what man thou com'st, and what thy quarrel.
        Speak truly on thy knighthood and thy oath,
        As so defend thee heaven and thy valour!   15

MOWB.   My name is Thomas Mowbray, Duke of Norfolk,
        Who hither come engaged by my oath
        (Which God defend a knight should violate!)
        Both to defend my loyalty and truth
        To God, my King, and his succeeding issue   20
        Against the Duke of Hereford that appeals me;
        And, by the grace of God and this mine arm,
        To prove him, in defending of myself,
        A traitor to my God, my King, and me;
        And as I truly fight, defend me heaven!   25

                    The trumpets sound. Enter [Boling-
                    broke], *Duke of Hereford, appellant,
                    in armour, and* Herald.

KING.   Marshal, ask yonder knight in arms
        Both who he is and why he cometh hither
        Thus plated in habiliments of war;
        And formally, according to our law,
        Depose him in the justice of his cause.   30

MAR.   What is thy name? and wherefore com'st thou hither,
        Before King Richard in his royal lists?
        Against whom comest thou? and what's thy quarrel?
        Speak like a true knight, so defend thee heaven!

---

9 *orderly* according to the rules.   13 *quarrel* cause in which you come.   17 *en-gaged* pledged.   18 *defend* forbid.   20 *his* F¹; Q¹: "my" is preferred by some editors.   21 *appeals* accuses.   25 *truly* in a just cause.   28 *plated* armoured. 30 *Depose him* take his oath.   45 *fair designs* orderly proceedings.   57 *blood*

BOLING. Harry of Hereford, Lancaster, and Derby   35
         Am I, who ready here do stand in arms
         To prove, by God's grace and my body's valour
         In lists on Thomas Mowbray, Duke of Norfolk,
         That he is a traitor, foul and dangerous,
         To God of heaven, King Richard, and to me;   40
         And as I truly fight, defend me heaven!
MAR.   On pain of death, no person be so bold
         Or daring-hardy as to touch the lists,
         Except the Marshal and such officers
         Appointed to direct these fair designs.   45

BOLING. Lord Marshal, let me kiss my sovereign's hand
         And bow my knee before his Majesty;
         For Mowbray and myself are like two men
         That vow a long and weary pilgrimage.
         Then let us take a ceremonious leave   50
         And loving farewell of our several friends.

MAR.   The appellant in all duty greets your Highness
         And craves to kiss your hand and take his leave.

KING.   We will descend and fold him in our arms.
         Cousin of Hereford, as thy cause is right,   55
         So be thy fortune in this royal fight!
         Farewell, my blood; which if to-day thou shed,
         Lament we may, but not revenge thee dead.

BOLING. O, let no noble eye profane a tear
         For me, if I be gor'd with Mowbray's spear.   60
         As confident as is the falcon's flight
         Against a bird, do I with Mowbray fight.
         My loving lord, I take my leave of you;
         Of you, my noble cousin, Lord Aumerle;
         Not sick, although I have to do with death,   65
         But lusty, young, and cheerly drawing breath.
         Lo, as at English feasts, so I regreet

---

kinsman.   59 *profane* Because Bolingbroke's death would indicate that he was a
traitor, to weep for him would be profanation.   66 *lusty* vigorous.   *cheerly*
cheerily.   67 *English feasts* These customarily concluded with elaborate sweet-
meats. *regreet* salute.

The daintiest last, to make the end most sweet.
O thou, the earthly author of my blood,
Whose youthful spirit, in me regenerate,   70
Doth with a twofold vigour lift me up
To reach at victory above my head,
Add proof unto mine armour with thy prayers,
And with thy blessings steel my lance's point,
That it may enter Mowbray's waxen coat   75
And furbish new the name of John a Gaunt
Even in the lusty haviour of his son.

GAUNT.   God in thy good cause make thee prosperous!
Be swift like lightning in the execution
And let thy blows, doubly redoubled,   80
Fall like amazing thunder on the casque
Of thy adverse pernicious enemy.
Rouse up thy youthful blood; be valiant and live.

BOLING. Mine innocency and Saint George to thrive!

MOWB.   However God or fortune cast my lot,   85
There lives or dies, true to King Richard's throne,
A loyal, just, and upright gentleman.
Never did captive with a freer heart
Cast off his chains of bondage and embrace
His golden uncontroll'd enfranchisement,   90
More than my dancing soul doth celebrate
This feast of battle with mine adversary.
Most mighty liege, and my companion peers,
Take from my mouth the wish of happy years.
As gentle and as jocund as to jest   95
Go I to fight. Truth hath a quiet breast.

KING.   Farewell, my lord. Securely I espy
Virtue with valour couched in thine eye.
Order the trial, Marshal, and begin.

---

69 *thou* John of Gaunt.   71 *twofold* not only with my own natural strength but
also with that which thou hadst when thou wert young [K].   73 *proof* strength to
resist weapons.   75 *waxen* soft, as though of wax.   76 *furbish new* add new
glory to.   77 *haviour* behaviour.   81 *amazing* stupefying. *casque* helmet.   84
innocency QQ; F1: "innocence." *to thrive* for my success.   85 *cast* determine.
88 *freer* more free from care.   90 *uncontroll'd enfranchisement* freedom from con-

MAR.   Harry of Hereford, Lancaster, and Derby,   100
          Receive thy lance, and God defend the right!

BOLING.   Strong as a tower in hope, I cry amen.

MAR.   [*to an* Officer] Go bear this lance to Thomas, Duke of
          Norfolk.

1. HERALD. Harry of Hereford, Lancaster, and Derby
          Stands here for God, his sovereign, and himself,   105
          On pain to be found false and recreant,
          To prove the Duke of Norfolk, Thomas Mowbray,
          A traitor to his God, his King, and him,
          And dares him to set forward to the fight.

2. HERALD. Here standeth Thomas Mowbray, Duke of Norfolk,   110
          On pain to be found false and recreant,
          Both to defend himself and to approve
          Henry of Hereford, Lancaster, and Derby
          To God, his sovereign, and to him disloyal,
          Courageously and with a free desire   115
          Attending but the signal to begin.

MAR.   Sound trumpets, and set forward combatants.

                              A charge sounded.

          Stay! The King hath thrown his warder down.

KING.   Let them lay by their helmets and their spears
          And both return back to their chairs again.   120
          Withdraw with us; and let the trumpets sound
          While we return these dukes what we decree.

                              A long flourish.

          Draw near,
          And list what with our Council we have done.
          For that our kingdom's earth should not be soil'd   125

---

trol or captivity.   92 *feast* festivity.   95 *gentle* calm in mind.   97 *Securely I
espy* I am confident that I see.   98 *couched* expressed.   112 *approve* prove.
116 *Attending* awaiting.   118 *warder* staff or truncheon, carried by the King as
supreme judge of the combat. To throw it down is to order a halt.   122 *while*
until.   *return* announce to.   124 *list* listen to   125 *For* in order.

With that dear blood which it hath fostered;
And for our eyes do hate the dire aspect
Of civil wounds plough'd up with neighbours' sword;
And for we think the eagle-winged pride
Of sky-aspiring and ambitious thoughts   130
With rival-hating envy set on you
To wake our peace, which in our country's cradle
Draws the sweet infant breath of gentle sleep;
Which so rous'd up with boist'rous untun'd drums,
With harsh-resounding trumpets' dreadful bray   135
And grating shock of wrathful iron arms,
Might from our quiet confines fright fair peace
And make us wade even in our kindred's blood:
Therefore we banish you our territories.
You, cousin Hereford, upon pain of life,   140
Till twice five summers have enrich'd our fields
Shall not regreet our fair dominions
But tread the stranger paths of banishment.

BOLING. Your will be done. This must my comfort be —
That sun that warms you here shall shine on me,   145
And those his golden beams to you here lent
Shall point on me and gild my banishment.

KING.   Norfolk, for thee remains a heavier doom,
Which I with some unwillingness pronounce:
The sly-slow hours shall not determinate   150
The dateless limit of thy dear exile.
The hopeless word of "never to return"
Breathe I against thee, upon pain of life.

MOWB.   A heavy sentence, my most sovereign liege,
And all unlook'd for from your Highness' mouth.   155

---

127 *for* because.   131 *envy* enmity. *set on you* set you on.   132 *wake* disturb.
134 *which* i.e. peace.   142 *regreet* greet again, return to.   143 *tread* . . . *banish-ment* wander as an exile in alien (stranger) lands.   146 *lent* afforded.   147 *point on* aim themselves at.   150 *sly-slow* creeping so slowly along that their passage is almost imperceptible [K]. *determinate* bring to an end.   151 *dateless limit* limitless period. *dear* grievous.   155 *unlook'd for* Mowbray had expected Richard to support him in his antagonism to Bolingbroke, whose ambition the King had good reason to fear [K].   156 *dearer merit* better recompense for past services. *maim* injury.   159 *forty years* Mowbray was only 33 years old at the time of his

A dearer merit, not so deep a maim
As to be cast forth in the common air,
Have I deserved at your Highness' hands.
The language I have learnt these forty years,
My native English, now I must forgo;   160
And now my tongue's use is to me no more
Than an unstringed viol or a harp,
Or like a cunning instrument cas'd up
Or, being open, put into his hands
That knows no touch to tune the harmony.   165
Within my mouth you have enjail'd my tongue,
Doubly portcullis'd with my teeth and lips;
And dull, unfeeling, barren ignorance
Is made my jailer to attend on me.
I am too old to fawn upon a nurse,   170
Too far in years to be a pupil now.
What is thy sentence then but speechless death,
Which robs my tongue from breathing native breath?

KING.   It boots thee not to be compassionate.
         After our sentence plaining comes too late.   175

MOWB.   Then thus I turn me from my country's light
         To dwell in solemn shades of endless night.

KING.   Return again and take an oath with thee.
         Lay on our royal sword your banish'd hands;
         Swear by the duty that you owe to God   180
         (Our part therein we banish with yourselves)
         To keep the oath that we administer:
         You never shall, so help you truth and God,
         Embrace each other's love in banishment;
         Nor never look upon each other's face;   185
         Nor never write, regreet, nor reconcile

---

banishment.   160 *forgo* give up.   163 *cunning* skillfully constructed.   164 *open*
out of its case.   167 *portcullis'd* enclosed by a movable grating, like the entrances
of medieval castles.   171 *be a pupil* learn to speak.   172 *then* F¹; not in QQ.
173 *which* i.e. thy sentence. *breathing native breath* (a) speaking my native language (b) breathing my native air.   174 *boots* avails.   *be compassionate* express
pity in emotional language.   175 *plaining* protest, lamentation.   179 *sword*
on the cross formed by the swordhilt.   181 *Our part therein* your allegiance.
Thus the King scornfully releases them from their allegiance during the term of
their banishment [K].

This low'ring tempest of your home-bred hate;
Nor never by advised purpose meet
To plot, contrive, or complot any ill
'Gainst us, our state, our subjects, or our land.   190

BOLING. I swear.

MOWB.   And I, to keep all this.

BOLING. Norfolk, so far as to mine enemy:
By this time, had the King permitted us,
One of our souls had wand'red in the air,   195
Banish'd this frail sepulchre of our flesh,
As now our flesh is banish'd from this land.
Confess thy treasons ere thou fly the realm.
Since thou hast far to go, bear not along
The clogging burden of a guilty soul.   200

MOWB.   No, Bolingbroke. If ever I were traitor,
My name be blotted from the book of life
And I from heaven banish'd as from hence!
But what thou art, God, thou, and I do know;
And all too soon, I fear, the King shall rue.   205
Farewell, my liege. Now no way can I stray.
Save back to England, all the world's my way.   *Exit.*

KING.   Uncle, even in the glasses of thine eyes
I see thy grieved heart. Thy sad aspect
Hath from the number of his banish'd years
Pluck'd four away. [*To* Bolingbroke] Six frozen winters
     spent,   210
Return with welcome home from banishment.

BOLING. How long a time lies in one little word!

---

187 *low'ring* threatening.   188 *by advised purpose* with deliberate intent.   190
state government.   193 *so . . . enemy* I have thus much to say to you at parting
—and I speak to you as an enemy (for my oath binds me not to make friends
with you), though my advice is that which a friend might well give [K]. *Far* F⁴; F¹,
QQ: "fare." The F⁴ reading has been accepted by most editors, although the line
has been interpreted in various ways.   200 *clogging* burdening.   205 *shall rue*
will learn to his sorrow.   206–7 *Now . . . way* I can never go astray except by
returning to England; the rest of the world is my road.   208 *glasses* mirrors.
211 *spent* having passed.   214 *wanton* sportive.   216 *in regard of* out of regard

Four lagging winters and four wanton springs
End in a word, such is the breath of kings.   215

GAUNT. I thank my liege that in regard of me
He shortens four years of my son's exile.
But little vantage shall I reap thereby;
For ere the six years that he hath to spend
Can change their moons and bring their times about,   220
My oil-dried lamp and time-bewasted light
Shall be extinct with age and endless night,
My inch of taper will be burnt and done,
And blindfold death not let me see my son.

KING. Why, uncle, thou hast many years to live.   225

GAUNT. But not a minute, King, that thou canst give.
Shorten my days thou canst with sullen sorrow
And pluck nights from me, but not lend a morrow.
Thou canst help time to furrow me with age,
But stop no wrinkle in his pilgrimage.   230
Thy word is current with him for my death,
But dead, thy kingdom cannot buy my breath.

KING. Thy son is banish'd upon good advice,
Whereto thy tongue a party-verdict gave.
Why at our justice seem'st thou then to low'r?   235

GAUNT. Things sweet to taste prove in digestion sour.
You urg'd me as a judge; but I had rather
You would have bid me argue like a father.
O, had it been a stranger, not my child,
To smooth his fault I should have been more mild.   240
A partial slander sought I to avoid,

---

for.   218 *vantage* profit.   222 *extinct* extinguished.   224 *blindfold* unseeing.
The traditional figure of death as the eyeless skull may here be fused with the
Greek conception of Atropos, the blindfolded destiny who cuts the thread of
life.   228 *morrow* morning.   230 *stop . . . pilgrimage* prevent no wrinkle which
the passage of time brings.   231 *current* valid.   234 *whereto . . . gave* in making
which decision you had a share.   237 *urg'd me* called on me for an opinion.
240 *smooth* palliate, extenuate.   241 *partial slander* reproach (slander) of par-
tiality.

And in the sentence my own life destroy'd.
Alas, I look'd when some of you should say
I was too strict to make mine own away;
But you gave leave to my unwilling tongue   245
Against my will to do myself this wrong.

KING.   Cousin, farewell; and, uncle, bid him so.
Six years we banish him, and he shall go.

Flourish. Exit [King *with his* Train].

AUM.   Cousin, farewell. What presence must not know,
From where you do remain let paper show.   250

MAR.   My lord, no leave take I; for I will ride,
As far as land will let me, by your side.

GAUNT.   O, to what purpose dost thou hoard thy words
That thou returnest no greeting to thy friends?

BOLING.   I have too few to take my leave of you,   255
When the tongue's office should be prodigal
To breathe the abundant dolour of the heart.

GAUNT.   Thy grief is but thy absence for a time.

BOLING.   Joy absent, grief is present for that time.

GAUNT.   What is six winters? They are quickly gone.   260

BOLING.   To men in joy; but grief makes one hour ten.

GAUNT.   Call it a travel that thou tak'st for pleasure.

BOLING.   My heart will sigh when I miscall it so,
Which finds it an enforced pilgrimage.

GAUNT.   The sullen passage of thy weary steps   265
Esteem as foil wherein thou art to set
The precious jewel of thy home return.

244 *strict* severely conscientious. *to make* in making.   *mine own* (a) my son (b)
my life.   246 *wrong* injury (not "injustice").   249 *What . . . know* what we
cannot learn from you in person.   250 *paper* letters.   256 *office* function.   257
breathe express. *dolour* grief.   265 *sullen* slow and melancholy.   266 *foil* leaf
of metal placed under a gem to enhance its brilliance by contrast.   269 *remember*
remind.   271 *apprenticehood* The regular term of an Elizabethan apprentice was
seven years.   272 *foreign passages* ways of life in foreign countries.   273 *freedom*
(a) discharge from apprenticeship (b) freedom from banishment.   274 *journeyman*

BOLING.   Nay, rather every tedious stride I make
          Will but remember me what a deal of world
          I wander from the jewels that I love.   270
          Must I not serve a long apprenticehood
          To foreign passages and, in the end,
          Having my freedom, boast of nothing else
          But that I was a journeyman to grief?

GAUNT.   All places that the eye of heaven visits   275
          Are to a wise man ports and happy havens.
          Teach thy necessity to reason thus:
          There is no virtue like necessity.
          Think not the King did banish thee,
          But thou the King. Woe doth the heavier sit   280
          Where it perceives it is but faintly borne.
          Go, say I sent thee forth to purchase honour,
          And not, the King exil'd thee; or suppose
          Devouring pestilence hangs in our air
          And thou art flying to a fresher clime.   285
          Look, what thy soul holds dear, imagine it
          To lie that way thou goest, not whence thou com'st.
          Suppose the singing birds musicians,
          The grass whereon thou tread'st the presence strow'd,
          The flowers fair ladies, and thy steps no more   290
          Than a delightful measure or a dance;
          For gnarling sorrow hath less power to bite
          The man that mocks at it and sets it light.

BOLING.   O, who can hold a fire in his hand
          By thinking on the frosty Caucasus?   295
          Or cloy the hungry edge of appetite
          By bare imagination of a feast?

---

to grief (a) one who has learned the trade of suffering (b) one who has travelled
with sorrow. The sense of the extended metaphor is that after he has served his
apprenticeship among foreign peoples the only trade he will have learned will be
that of suffering.   278 *necessity* the patient enduring of the inevitable.   281
faintly faint-heartedly.   282 *purchase* win.   286 *what* whatever.   289 *presence*
king's presence chamber.   *strow'd* strewn with rushes, as was the fashion in Elizabethan houses.   291 *measure* a stately, formal figure or movement in dancing.
292 *gnarling* growling.   296 *cloy* satisfy.

Or wallow naked in December snow
By thinking on fantastic summer's heat?
O, no! The apprehension of the good   300
Gives but the greater feeling to the worse.
Fell sorrow's tooth doth never rankle more
Than when he bites, but lanceth not the sore.

GAUNT.   Come, come, my son, I'll bring thee on thy way.
Had I thy youth and cause, I would not stay.   305

BOLING. Then, England's ground, farewell; sweet soil, adieu,
My mother, and my nurse, that bears me yet!
Where'er I wander, boast of this I can,
Though banish'd, yet a trueborn English man. *Exeunt.*

◇◇◇◇◇◇◇◇◇◇◇◇◇◇◇◇◇◇

SCENE IV. [*London. The court.*]

Enter the King, *with* Green *and* Bagot, *at one door,
and the* Lord Aumerle *at another.*

KING.   We did observe. Cousin Aumerle,
How far brought you high Hereford on his way?

AUM.   I brought high Hereford, if you call him so,
But to the next high way, and there I left him.

KING.   And say, what store of parting tears were shed?   5

AUM.   Faith, none for me; except the northeast wind,
Which then blew bitterly against our faces,
Awak'd the sleeping rheum, and so by chance
Did grace our hollow parting with a tear.

KING.   What said our cousin when you parted with him?   10

---

299 *fantastic* imaginary.   300–1 *apprehension . . . worse* the mind's conception
(the idea) of what is good merely gives more poignancy to discomfort or mis-
fortune [K].   302 *Fell* fierce.   303 *lanceth* as a surgeon lances a wound to cure
the patient.   304 *bring* escort.   305 *stay* linger.
    I.IV. 2 *brought* accompanied.   6 *for me* on my part. *except* unless perhaps.   8
sleeping rheum dormant moisture, tears.   9 *hollow* insincere.   12 *for* because.
13 *that* that fact, my heart's disdain.   14 *counterfeit* pretend.   *oppression of*

AUM.   "Farewell!"
        And, for my heart disdained that my tongue
        Should so profane the word, that taught me craft
        To counterfeit oppression of such grief
        That words seem'd buried in my sorrow's grave.   15
        Marry, would the word "farewell" have length'ned hours
        And added years to his short banishment,
        He should have had a volume of farewells;
        But since it would not, he had none of me.

KING.   He is our cousin, cousin; but 'tis doubt,   20
        When time shall call him home from banishment,
        Whether our kinsman come to see his friends.
        Ourself and Bushy, Bagot here, and Green
        Observ'd his courtship to the common people;
        How he did seem to dive into their hearts   25
        With humble and familiar courtesy;
        What reverence he did throw away on slaves,
        Wooing poor craftsmen with the craft of smiles
        And patient underbearing of his fortune,
        As 'twere to banish their affects with him.   30
        Off goes his bonnet to an oyster-wench;
        A brace of draymen bid God speed him well
        And had the tribute of his supple knee,
        With "Thanks, my countrymen, my loving friends";
        As were our England in reversion his,   35
        And he our subjects' next degree in hope.

GREEN. Well, he is gone, and with him go these thoughts!
        Now for the rebels which stand out in Ireland,
        Expedient manage must be made, my liege,
        Ere further leisure yield them further means   40
        For their advantage and your Highness' loss.

that I was oppressed with.   20 *cousin, cousin* F¹; QQ: "cousin's cousin."   22 *to
see his friends* The King suspects that Bolingbroke will return as an enemy [K].
29 *patient underbearing* calm enduring.   30 *As 'twere . . .
him* as if he were
trying to carry the affections of the common people away with him in his
banishment [K].   32 *brace* pair.   35 *in reversion* by right of legal succession.
36 *next degree in hope* nearest heir to the throne.   38 *stand out* are in rebellion.   39 *Expedient* speedy. *manage* arrangements.

KING.   We will ourself in person to this war;
          And, for our coffers, with too great a court
          And liberal largess, are grown somewhat light,
          We are enforc'd to farm our royal realm,   45
          The revenue whereof shall furnish us
          For our affairs in hand. If that come short,
          Our substitutes at home shall have blank charters,
          Whereto, when they shall know what men are rich,
          They shall subscribe them for large sums of gold   50
          And send them after to supply our wants,
          For we will make for Ireland presently.

                        Enter Bushy.

          Bushy, what news?

BUSHY.   Old John of Gaunt is grievous sick, my lord,
          Suddenly taken, and hath sent post-haste   55
          To entreat your Majesty to visit him.

KING.   Where lies he?

BUSHY.   At Ely House.

KING.   Now put it, God, in the physician's mind
          To help him to his grave immediately!   60
          The lining of his coffers shall make coats
          To deck our soldiers for these Irish wars.
          Come, gentlemen, let's all go visit him.
          Pray God we may make haste, and come too late!

ALL.   Amen.   *Exeunt.*

---

42 *to* go to.   43 *for* because.   43 *too great a court* too many retainers. Richard
was noted for the extravagance of his court.   44 *liberal largess* lavish gifts.   45
farm . . . realm grant to certain lords, in exchange for immediate cash, the right
to collect taxes. This money-raising device was particularly resented by Richard's
subjects.   48 *substitutes at home* deputies left to govern in my absence.
blank charters papers which wealthy persons were required to sign as promises
to pay, with the specific amount left blank so as to be filled in however the king
desired. This was another very obnoxious means of raising money.   50 *subscribe
them* put them down.   52 *presently* immediately.   53 *Bushy, what news* F¹; not
in QQ.   58 *Ely House* the Bishop of Ely's palace in Holborn, where Gaunt died.
61 *lining* (a) contents (b) coat lining.   *coats* coats of mail.

Act Two

<><><><><><><><><><><><><><><><><><><><><><><><><><><><><><><><><><><><>

SCENE I. [*London. Ely House.*]

Enter John of Gaunt, *sick, with the* Duke of York &c.

GAUNT. Will the King come, that I may breathe my last
In wholesome counsel to his unstaid youth?

YORK. Vex not yourself nor strive not with your breath,
For all in vain comes counsel to his ear.

GAUNT. O, but they say the tongues of dying men   5
Enforce attention like deep harmony.
Where words are scarce, they are seldom spent in vain,
For they breathe truth that breathe their words in pain.
He that no more must say is listened more
    Than they whom youth and ease have taught to glose.   10
More are men's ends mark'd than their lives before.
    The setting sun, and music at the close,
As the last taste of sweets, is sweetest last,
Writ in remembrance more than things long past.
Though Richard my life's counsel would not hear,   15
My death's sad tale may yet undeaf his ear.

YORK. No; it is stopp'd with other flattering sounds,
As praises, of whose taste the wise are fond,

II.i. 8 *breathe* speak.   10 *glose* speak empty words of flattery.   12 *close* the con-
clusion of a musical phrase, theme, or movement.   14 *writ in remembrance* set
down (as if in writing) in the memory.   15 *life's counsel* advice when I was
alive.   16 *My death's sad tale* the serious (sad) words I speak on my deathbed.
18 *of . . . fond* of whose taste even the wise are (a) fond (b) made foolish. *fond*
COLLIER; Q¹: "found."   19 *metres* songs. *venom* poisonous.

25

Lascivious metres, to whose venom sound
The open ear of youth doth always listen;   20
Report of fashions in proud Italy,
Whose manners still our tardy apish nation
Limps after in base imitation.
Where doth the world thrust forth a vanity
(So it be new, there's no respect how vile)   25
That is not quickly buzz'd into his ears?
Then all too late comes counsel to be heard
Where will doth mutiny with wit's regard.
Direct not him whose way himself will choose.
'Tis breath thou lack'st, and that breath wilt thou lose.   30

GAUNT. Methinks I am a prophet new inspir'd
And thus, expiring, do foretell of him:
His rash fierce blaze of riot cannot last,
For violent fires soon burn out themselves;
Small show'rs last long, but sudden storms are short;   35
He tires betimes that spurs too fast betimes;
With eager feeding food doth choke the feeder;
Light vanity, insatiate cormorant,
Consuming means, soon preys upon itself.
This royal throne of kings, this scept'red isle,   40
This earth of majesty, this seat of Mars,
This other Eden, demi-paradise,
This fortress built by Nature for herself
Against infection and the hand of war,
This happy breed of men, this little world,   45
This precious stone set in the silver sea,
Which serves it in the office of a wall,
Or as a moat defensive to a house,

---

21 *proud* lavish, particularly with regard to elegant clothes.   22 *still* always.
tardy apish imitative.   24 *thrust forth a vanity* exhibit any piece of showy extravagance — any idle fashion in life or conduct [K].   25 *So* provided that.
there's no respect it makes no difference. *vile* contemptible.   28 *Where* will . . .
regard where one's desires rise in rebellion against all considerations of wisdom or
common sense [K]. 29 *whose . . . choose* who insists on choosing his own course
(having his own way) regardless of advice [K].   33 *rash* quickly kindled and burn-
ing rapidly. *riot* dissipation.   36 *He . . . betimes* he soon tires who rides too fast
early in the day — at the beginning of the day's travel [K].   38-9 *Light . . . itself*
a life of reckless prodigality soon uses up the means of life (one's "living") and

Against the envy of less happier lands;
This blessed plot, this earth, this realm, this England,   50
This nurse, this teeming womb of royal kings,
Fear'd by their breed and famous by their birth,
Renowned for their deeds as far from home,
For Christian service and true chivalry,
As is the sepulchre in stubborn Jewry   55
Of the world's ransom, blessed Mary's son;
This land of such dear souls, this dear dear land,
Dear for her reputation through the world,
Is now leas'd out (I die pronouncing it)
Like to a tenement or pelting farm.   60
England, bound in with the triumphant sea,
Whose rocky shore beats back the envious siege
Of wat'ry Neptune, is now bound in with shame,
With inky blots and rotten parchment bonds.
That England that was wont to conquer others   65
Hath made a shameful conquest of itself.
Ah, would the scandal vanish with my life,
How happy then were my ensuing death!

Enter King, Queen, Aumerle, Bushy,
Green, Bagot, Ross, *and* Willoughby.

YORK.   The King is come. Deal mildly with his youth;
For young hot colts, being rag'd, do rage the more.   70

QUEEN.   How fares our noble uncle Lancaster?

KING.   What comfort, man? How is't with aged Gaunt?

GAUNT.   O, how that name befits my composition!
Old Gaunt indeed, and gaunt in being old.

---

thus wears itself out for lack of sustenance. Gaunt is thinking of spendthrifts who,
having outrun their income, sacrifice their principal and are left with nothing to
live on [K].   44 *infection* both moral (degenerate foreign customs) and physical
(invasion) polution from other lands.   47 *office* function.   49 *envy* enmity.   52
by their breed because of their warlike ancestry.   55 *stubborn* (a) resisting conquest (b) rejecting Christ. *Jewry* Judæa.   56 *ransom* redeemer.   60 *tenement*
rented land or building. *pelting* paltry, insignificant.   62 *envious* hostile.   70
rag'd (a) enraged (b) roughly handled.   73 *composition* constitution, body and
mind.

Within me grief hath kept a tedious fast;   75
And who abstains from meat that is not gaunt?
For sleeping England long time have I watch'd;
Watching breeds leanness, leanness is all gaunt.
The pleasure that some fathers feed upon
Is my strict fast — I mean my children's looks —   80
And therein fasting hast thou made me gaunt.
Gaunt am I for the grave, gaunt as a grave,
Whose hollow womb inherits naught but bones.

KING.   Can sick men play so nicely with their names?

GAUNT.   No, misery makes sport to mock itself.   85
          Since thou dost seek to kill my name in me,
          I mock my name, great King, to flatter thee.

KING.   Should dying men flatter with those that live?

GAUNT.   No, no! men living flatter those that die.

KING.   Thou, now a-dying, say'st thou flatterest me.   90

GAUNT.   O, no! thou diest, though I the sicker be.

KING.   I am in health, I breathe, and see thee ill.

GAUNT.   Now, he that made me knows I see thee ill;
          Ill in myself to see, and in thee seeing ill.
          Thy deathbed is no lesser than thy land,   95
          Wherein thou liest in reputation sick;
          And thou, too careless patient as thou art,
          Committ'st thy anointed body to the cure
          Of those physicians that first wounded thee.
          A thousand flatterers sit within thy crown,   100

75 *kept . . . fast* caused me to fast.   76 *meat* food.   77 *watch'd* kept awake,
gone without sleep.   78 *Watching* sleeplessness.   80 *strict fast* that from which
I have been forced to abstain.   83 *inherits* possesses.   84 *play* pun. *nicely* (a)
subtly (b) foolishly.   85 *to mock* of mocking.   86 *kill my name in me* to make
my name die with me by depriving me of my heir, since my son is banished
[κ].   88 *flatter with* seek to please.   94 *Ill . . . ill* made sick at heart by the
sight of thy illness, discerning as I do the malady from which thou sufferest [κ].
102 *incaged* F¹; QQ: "inraged."   *verge* (a) boundary (b) metal rim of the
crown.   104 *grandsire* Edward III.   105 *son's son* Richard, son of the Black
Prince.   *his* Edward III's.   107 *wert possess'd* came into possession (of the throne).
108 *possess'd* insane (possessed by devils).   109 *regent* ruler.   111 *for thy world*
as thy entire domain.   113 *now, not* THEOBALD; Q¹: "now, not, not."   114 *Thy*

Whose compass is no bigger than thy head;
And yet, incaged in so small a verge,
The waste is no whit lesser than thy land.
O, had thy grandsire, with a prophet's eye,
Seen how his son's son should destroy his sons,   105
From forth thy reach he would have laid thy shame,
Deposing thee before thou wert possess'd,
Which art possess'd now to depose thyself.
Why, cousin, wert thou regent of the world,
It were a shame to let this land by lease;   110
But, for thy world enjoying but this land,
Is it not more than shame to shame it so?
Landlord of England art thou now, not King.
Thy state of law is bondslave to the law,
And thou —

KING.   A lunatic lean-witted fool,   115
Presuming on an ague's privilege,
Dar'st with thy frozen admonition
Make pale our cheek, chasing the royal blood
With fury from his native residence.
Now, by my seat's right royal majesty,   120
Wert thou not brother to great Edward's son,
This tongue that runs so roundly in thy head
Should run thy head from thy unreverent shoulders.

GAUNT.   O, spare me not, my brother Edward's son,
For that I was his father Edward's son!   125
That blood already, like the pelican,
Hast thou tapp'd out and drunkenly carous'd.

. . . *law* your legal status is no longer that of supreme King of England by divine
right; for you are now as subject to the law in regard to the whole realm as any
landlord is with reference to his private estate when he has given a lease of it [K].
116 *ague's privilege* the liberty in speech of a man suffering from a minor
illness, fever and chills.   117 *frozen* (a) frigid (b) prompted by a chill, such as
one with an ague would suffer.   121 *great Edward's son* the Black Prince, Richard's father.   122 *roundly* freely and bluntly.   125 *For that* because.   126 *pelican* bird reputed to feed its children with its own blood. The parent pelican was
a conventional symbol of self-sacrifice, often identified with Christ in Elizabethan
emblem books. The young pelican, to which Richard is compared, was a symbol
of unfilial ingratitude.   127 *tapp'd out* by the murder of Gloucester. *carous'd*
drunk in great draughts.

My brother Gloucester, plain well-meaning soul
(Whom fair befall in heaven 'mongst happy souls!),
May be a precedent and witness good   130
That thou respect'st not spilling Edward's blood.
Join with the present sickness that I have,
And thy unkindness be like crooked age,
To crop at once a too long withered flower.
Live in thy shame, but die not shame with thee!   135
These words hereafter thy tormenters be!
Convey me to my bed, then to my grave.
Love they to live that love and honour have.

> *Exit* [*borne off by* Attendants].

KING. And let them die that age and sullens have;
For both hast thou, and both become the grave.   140

YORK. I do beseech your Majesty, impute his words
To wayward sickliness and age in him.
He loves you, on my life, and holds you dear
As Harry Duke of Hereford, were he here.

KING. Right, you say true! As Hereford's love, so his; 145
As theirs, so mine; and all be as it is!

> *Enter* Northumberland.

NORTH. My liege, old Gaunt commends him to your Majesty.

KING. What says he?

NORTH.   Nay, nothing; all is said.
His tongue is now a stringless instrument;
Words, life, and all, old Lancaster hath spent.   150

YORK. Be York the next that must be bankrout so!
Though death be poor, it ends a mortal woe.

KING. The ripest fruit first falls, and so doth he;

---

129 *fair befall* may good befall.   130 *precedent* proof.   131 *respect'st not* feel no
scruples about.   133 *crooked* bent like a sickle.   139 *sullens* sulks.   140 *become*
are fit for.   147 *commends him* sends his greetings.   151 *bankrout* bankrupt,
by having spent words, life and all.   152 *poor* The metaphor of death as bank-
ruptcy is continued.   154 *must be* is yet to be accomplished.   156 *supplant* drive
out.   *rug-headed* shaggy-haired.   *kerns* light-armed Irish footsoldiers.   157–8 *which
. . . live* referring to the legend that St. Patrick had banished the snakes from

His time is spent, our pilgrimage must be.
So much for that. Now for our Irish wars.   155
We must supplant those rough rug-headed kerns,
Which live like venom where no venom else
But only they have privilege to live.
And, for these great affairs do ask some charge,
Towards our assistance we do seize to us   160
The plate, coin, revenues, and moveables
Whereof our uncle Gaunt did stand possess'd.

YORK.   How long shall I be patient? Ah, how long
Shall tender duty make me suffer wrong?
Not Gloucester's death, nor Hereford's banishment,   165
Nor Gaunt's rebukes, nor England's private wrongs,
Nor the prevention of poor Bolingbroke
About his marriage, nor my own disgrace,
Have ever made me sour my patient cheek
Or bend one wrinkle on my sovereign's face.   170
I am the last of noble Edward's sons,
Of whom thy father, Prince of Wales, was first.
In war was never lion rag'd more fierce,
In peace was never gentle lamb more mild,
Than was that young and princely gentleman.   175
His face thou hast, for even so look'd he,
Accomplish'd with the number of thy hours;
But when he frown'd, it was against the French
And not against his friends. His noble hand
Did win what he did spend, and spent not that   180
Which his triumphant father's hand had won.
His hands were guilty of no kindred blood,
But bloody with the enemies of his kin.
O Richard! York is too far gone with grief,
Or else he never would compare between.   185

Ireland. *venom* poisonous snakes.   159 *for* because.   *charge* expense.   161 *moveables* furniture, clothing and jewelry.   164 *tender duty* scrupulous regard for my duty to my King [K].   166 *Gaunt's rebukes* rebukes to Gaunt. *private* suffered by private citizens.   167-8 *prevention . . . marriage* Although the episode does not otherwise figure in this play, Holinshed reports that during Bolingbroke's exile Richard forestalled his marriage to the daughter of the Duc de Berri.   170 *bend one wrinkle* direct one frown.   177 *Accomplish'd . . . hours* at your age.

KING.   Why, uncle, what's the matter?

YORK.   O, my liege,
          Pardon me, if you please; if not, I, pleas'd
          Not to be pardoned, am content withal.
          Seek you to seize and gripe into your hands
          The royalties and rights of banish'd Hereford?   190
          Is not Gaunt dead? and doth not Hereford live?
          Was not Gaunt just? and is not Harry true?
          Did not the one deserve to have an heir?
          Is not his heir a well-deserving son?
          Take Hereford's rights away, and take from Time   195
          His charters and his customary rights;
          Let not to-morrow then ensue to-day;
          Be not thyself — for how art thou a king
          But by fair sequence and succession?
          Now, afore God (God forbid I say true!),   200
          If you do wrongfully seize Hereford's rights,
          Call in the letters patents that he hath
          By his attorneys general to sue
          His livery, and deny his off'red homage,
          You pluck a thousand dangers on your head,   205
          You lose a thousand well-disposed hearts,
          And prick my tender patience to those thoughts
          Which honour and allegiance cannot think.

KING.   Think what you will, we seize into our hands
          His plate, his goods, his money, and his lands.   210

YORK.   I'll not be by the while. My liege, farewell.
          What will ensue hereof there's none can tell;
          But by bad courses may be understood
          That their events can never fall out good.   *Exit.*

---

188 *withal* with not being pardoned.   189 *gripe* grasp.   190 *royalties* rights as a
member of the royal family.   195 *from Time* since Hereford's rights have come
to him by succession — in the inevitable course of time [K].   196 *His* Time's.
customary rights One of the rights of Time is to deliver his inheritance to the
heir.   197 *ensue* follow.   202 *Call in* revoke. *letters patents* royal grants.   203–4
By . . . livery the royal grant that gives him the right to make suit by means
of his attorneys general (persons to whom he gives power of attorney to represent
him all business) for the delivery of the lands that his father held as tenant of

KING.	Go, Bushy, to the Earl of Wiltshire straight. 215
	Bid him repair to us to Ely House
	To see this business. To-morrow next
	We will for Ireland; and 'tis time, I trow.
	And we create, in absence of ourself,
	Our uncle York Lord Governor of England; 220
	For he is just and always lov'd us well.
	Come on, our queen. To-morrow must we part.
	Be merry, for our time of stay is short.

Flourish. Exeunt. Manent Northumberland, Willoughby, *and* Ross.

NORTH. Well, lords, the Duke of Lancaster is dead.

ROSS. And living too; for now his son is Duke.   225

WIL. Barely in title, not in revenues.

NORTH. Richly in both, if justice had her right.

ROSS. My heart is great; but it must break with silence,
Ere 't be disburdened with a liberal tongue.

NORTH. Nay, speak thy mind; and let him ne'er speak more   230
That speaks thy words again to do thee harm!

WIL. Tends that thou wouldst speak to the Duke of Hereford?
If it be so, out with it boldly, man!
Quick is mine ear to hear of good towards him.

ROSS. No good at all that I can do for him;   235
Unless you call it good to pity him,
Bereft and gelded of his patrimony.

NORTH. Now, afore God, 'tis shame such wrongs are borne
In him a royal prince and many moe
Of noble blood in this declining land.   240

---

the crown [K]. *livery* delivery.   204 *deny* refuse to accept.   *homage* For Bolingbroke to do homage to the King would be part of the ceremony attending the
delivery of the lands [K].   205 *pluck* pull down.   207 *prick* incite.   211 *by* present.
213 *by* by means of.   214 *events* results.   217 *see* see to.   218 *trow* believe.   226
Barely (a) scarcely (b) with bare title, for he has only the title and not the revenue.
228 *great* swollen (with grief and indignation).   232 *Tends . . . to* does that
which you wish to speak about concern.   237 *gelded* emasculated.   239 *moe*
more.

The King is not himself, but basely led
By flatterers; and what they will inform,
Merely in hate, 'gainst any of us all,
That will the King severely prosecute
'Gainst us, our lives, our children, and our heirs.   245

ROSS.   The commons hath he pill'd with grievous taxes
And quite lost their hearts; the nobles hath he fin'd
For ancient quarrels and quite lost their hearts.

WIL.   And daily new exactions are devis'd,
As blanks, benevolences, and I wot not what;   250
But what, a God's name, doth become of this?

NORTH.   Wars have not wasted it, for warr'd he hath not,
But basely yielded upon compromise
That which his noble ancestors achiev'd with blows.
More hath he spent in peace than they in wars.   255

ROSS.   The Earl of Wiltshire hath the realm in farm.

WIL.   The King's grown bankrout, like a broken man.

NORTH.   Reproach and dissolution hangeth over him.

ROSS.   He hath not money for these Irish wars,
His burdenous taxations notwithstanding,   260
But by the robbing of the banish'd Duke.

NORTH.   His noble kinsman. Most degenerate king!
But, lords, we hear this fearful tempest sing,
Yet seek no shelter to avoid the storm.
We see the wind sit sore upon our sails,   265

---

243 *Merely* purely.   244 *prosecute* follow up.   246 *pill'd* stripped bare, despoiled.
250 *blanks* the blank charters.   *benevolences* forced loans to the crown (he is
being ironic).   *wot* know.   251 *a* in.   *this* all this money.   253-4 *basely . . .
blows* The reference is to the treaty with Charles VI of France made in 1393
and renewed in 1396, by which Brest, won by Edward III and the Black Prince,
was yielded to the Duke of Brittany. This caused the original quarrel between
Richard and the Duke of Gloucester.   256 *in farm* on lease, with the rights of
tax collection.   257 *bankrout* bankrupt.   *broken* financially ruined.   258 *Reproach and dissolution* a shameful and fatal end of life [K].   260 *burdenous*
burdensome.   263 *sing* sound in the wind.   265 *sit sore* weigh heavily.   266 *strike*
(a) strike (lower) sail (b) strike back.   *securely* overconfidently, not heeding the
danger.   267 *wrack* shipwreck.   268 *unavoided* unavoidable, inevitable.   269

And yet we strike not, but securely perish.

ROSS.   We see the very wrack that we must suffer,
And unavoided is the danger now
For suffering so the causes of our wrack.

NORTH.   Not so. Even through the hollow eyes of death   270
I spy life peering; but I dare not say
How near the tidings of our comfort is.

WIL.   Nay, let us share thy thoughts as thou dost ours.

ROSS.   Be confident to speak, Northumberland.
We three are but thyself, and speaking so,   275
Thy words are but as thoughts. Therefore be bold.

NORTH.   Then thus: I have from Le Port Blanc, a bay
In Britain, receiv'd intelligence
That Harry Duke of Hereford, Rainold Lord Cobham,

.   280

That late broke from the Duke of Exeter,
His brother, Archbishop late of Canterbury,
Sir Thomas Erpingham, Sir John Ramston,
Sir John Norbery, Sir Robert Waterton, and Francis
Quoint,
All these well furnish'd by the Duke of Britain   285
With eight tall ships, three thousand men of war,
Are making hither with all due expedience
And shortly mean to touch our northern shore.
Perhaps they had ere this, but that they stay

For . . . wrack because we have thus allowed the causes of our ruin (the King's misrule) to go on unchecked [K]. *suffering* permitting.   *275-6 speaking . . . thoughts* when you speak under such conditions—that is, to persons who are, as it were, your other selves — your words are as safe from betrayal as if they were unspoken thoughts [K].   277 *Le Port Blanc* the modern Port le Blanc, near Tréguier, Côte du Nord.   278 *Britain* Brittany.   280 A line here has been lost. Since Shakespeare is following Holinshed in this list, we can surmise that it read something like "The son of Richard Earl of Arundel," in which case the line may have been deleted for political reasons, for the son of the Elizabethan Earl of Arundel had been imprisoned by Queen Elizabeth.   281 *broke* escaped. 282 *His* the Earl of Arundel's.   284 *Quoint* F¹; QQ: "Coines."   287 *due expedience* proper speed.   289 *had* would have.   *stay* await.

The first departing of the King for Ireland.   290
If then we shall shake off our slavish yoke,
Imp out our drooping country's broken wing,
Redeem from broking pawn the blemish'd crown,
Wipe off the dust that hides our sceptre's gilt,
And make high majesty look like itself,   295
Away with me in post to Ravenspurgh;
But if you faint, as fearing to do so,
Stay and be secret, and myself will go.

ROSS.   To horse, to horse! Urge doubts to them that fear.

WIL.   Hold out my horse, and I will first be there.   300

                                    Exeunt.

◇◇◇◇◇◇◇◇◇◇◇◇◇◇◇◇◇

SCENE II. [*Windsor Castle.*]

Enter the Queen, Bushy, Bagot.

BUSHY.   Madam, your Majesty is too much sad.
          You promis'd, when you parted with the King,
          To lay aside life-harming heaviness
          And entertain a cheerful disposition.

QUEEN.   To please the King, I did; to please myself,   5
          I cannot do it. Yet I know no cause
          Why I should welcome such a guest as grief
          Save bidding farewell to so sweet a guest
          As my sweet Richard. Yet again, methinks,

---

291 *shall* are to.   292 *Imp out* graft new feathers on (a technical term from falconry).   293 *from broking pawn* from being pledged to moneylenders.   294 *gilt* golden lustre.   296 *in post* at full speed. *Ravenspurgh* once the most important port on the Humber river, between Hull and Bridlington, but now submerged by the sea.   297 *faint* are faint-hearted.   299 *Urge* speak of.   300 *Hold out my horse* if my horse holds out.

   II.II.   3 *heaviness* melancholy.   11–12 *my inward . . . trembles* the very soul within me shudders, though I know no reason for fear. Such bitter soul-felt grief must have some cause besides my natural sorrow at parting from my husband [K]. 14 *Each . . . shadows* for every real cause for grief there are twenty imaginary ones.

Some unborn sorrow, ripe in fortune's womb,   10
Is coming towards me, and my inward soul
With nothing trembles. At something it grieves
More than with parting from my lord the King.

BUSHY. Each substance of a grief hath twenty shadows,
Which shows like grief itself, but is not so;   15
For sorrow's eye, glazed with blinding tears,
Divides one thing entire to many objects,
Like perspectives, which rightly gaz'd upon,
Show nothing but confusion — ey'd awry,
Distinguish form. So your sweet Majesty,   20
Looking awry upon your lord's departure,
Find shapes of grief more than himself to wail,
Which, look'd on as it is, is naught but shadows
Of what it is not. Then, thrice-gracious Queen,
More than your lord's departure weep not. More's not
    seen   25
Or if it be, 'tis with false sorrow's eye,
Which for things true weeps things imaginary.

QUEEN. It may be so; but yet my inward soul
Persuades me it is otherwise. Howe'er it be,
I cannot but be sad — so heavy sad   30
As, though in thinking on no thought I think,
Makes me with heavy nothing faint and shrink.

BUSHY. 'Tis nothing but conceit, my gracious lady.

QUEEN. 'Tis nothing less. Conceit is still deriv'd
From some forefather grief. Mine is not so,   35

---

15 *shows* appears.   16 *glazed* covered as with a glassy film.   18 *perspectives*
optical toys (raised pictures) popular in the Renaissance. Looked at directly, they
showed only confusion; from the side (awry) they revealed various pictures. The
point of the metaphor is that Isabel is not looking at Richard's departure from
the proper angle.   21 *awry* wrongly (with a quibble on "awry" of line 19, meaning "from the side").   22 *more than himself* in addition to the original cause for
grief.   31 *though . . . think* although I strive to think about nothing. *though*
F¹; Q¹: "thought."   32 *heavy nothing* sorrow without cause.   33 *conceit* imagination.   34 *nothing less* anything but that. *still* always.   35 *forefather grief*
actual grief experienced in the past.

For nothing hath begot my something grief,
Or something hath the nothing that I grieve.
'Tis in reversion that I do possess;
But what it is that is not yet known what,
I cannot name. 'Tis nameless woe, I wot.   40

Enter Green.

GREEN.   God save your Majesty! and well met, gentlemen.
I hope the King is not yet shipp'd for Ireland.

QUEEN.   Why hopest thou so? 'Tis better hope he is;
For his designs crave haste, his haste good hope.
Then wherefore dost thou hope he is not shipp'd?   45

GREEN.   That he, our hope, might have retir'd his power
And driven into despair an enemy's hope
Who strongly hath set footing in this land.
The banish'd Bolingbroke repeals himself
And with uplifted arms is safe arriv'd   50
At Ravenspurgh.

QUEEN.   Now God in heaven forbid!

GREEN.   Ah, madam, 'tis too true; and that is worse,
The Lord Northumberland, his son young Henry Percy,
The Lords of Ross, Beaumond, and Willoughby,
With all their powerful friends, are fled to him.   55

BUSHY.   Why have you not proclaim'd Northumberland
And all the rest revolted faction traitors?

GREEN.   We have; whereupon the Earl of Worcester
Hath broken his staff, resign'd his stewardship,
And all the household servants fled with him to
Bolingbroke.   60

---

37 *something . . . grieve* some actual cause of grief has produced a grief that
exists only in my imagination [K].   38 *'Tis in . . . possess* the grief that I feel
is like a reversionary interest in an estate — something will happen in the future
to account for it [K].   40 *wot* believe.   44 *crave* demand.   46 *retir'd his power*
drawn back his army.   48 *strongly* with strong support.   49 *repeals himself* calls
himself back from exile.   50 *uplifted* brandished.   52 *that* that which.   57 *all*
. . . faction all the others of the rebellious faction.   59 *staff* the sign of his office.
61 *midwife to my woe* since you have revealed the unknown cause of my
sorrow [K]. The childbirth metaphor of lines 9–12 is continued.   62 *dismal* ill-

QUEEN. So, Green, thou art the midwife to my woe,
        And Bolingbroke my sorrow's dismal heir.
        Now hath my soul brought forth her prodigy;
        And I, a gasping new-deliver'd mother,
        Have woe to woe, sorrow to sorrow join'd.   65

BUSHY. Despair not, madam.

QUEEN.   Who shall hinder me?
        I will despair, and be at enmity
        With cozening Hope. He is a flatterer,
        A parasite, a keeper-back of Death,
        Who gently would dissolve the bands of life,   70
        Which false hope lingers in extremity.

                    Enter York.

GREEN. Here comes the Duke of York.

QUEEN. With signs of war about his aged neck.
        O, full of careful business are his looks.
        Uncle, for God's sake, speak comfortable words!   75

YORK.   Should I do so, I should belie my thoughts.
        Comfort's in heaven, and we are on the earth,
        Where nothing lives but crosses, cares, and grief.
        Your husband, he is gone to save far off,
        Whilst others come to make him lose at home.   80
        Here am I left to underprop his land,
        Who, weak with age, cannot support myself.
        Now comes the sick hour that his surfeit made;
        Now shall he try his friends that flatter'd him.

                Enter a Servingman.

omened.   62 *heir* offspring.   63 *prodigy* monstrous child, Bolingbroke. She
is like a woman whose newborn infant is so monstrous a creature that his birth
does not relieve her sufferings but adds to them [K].   68 *cozening* deceitful.   70
bands bonds.   71 *lingers* postpones.   *in extremity* in extremis, when one is
at the point of death.   73 *signs of war* armour, a gorget, piece of mail used
to protect the throat.   74 *careful* distressful.   75 *comfortable* comforting.   78
crosses frustrations.   83 *surfeit* excess (in eating), riotous conduct as king.   84
try put to the test.

SERV.	My lord, your son was gone before I came.

85

YORK. He was? Why, so! Go all which way it will!
The nobles they are fled, the commons they are cold
And will, I fear, revolt on Hereford's side.
Sirrah, get thee to Plashy to my sister Gloucester;
Bid her send me presently a thousand pound.   90
Hold, take my ring.

SERV. My lord, I had forgot to tell your lordship
To-day, as I came by, I called there —
But I shall grieve you to report the rest.

YORK. What is't, knave?   95

SERV. An hour before I came the Duchess died.

YORK. God for his mercy! what a tide of woes
Comes rushing on this woeful land at once!
I know not what to do. I would to God
(So my untruth had not provok'd him to it)   100
The King had cut off my head with my brother's.
What, are there no posts dispatch'd for Ireland?
How shall we do for money for these wars?
Come, sister — cousin I would say — pray pardon me. —
Go, fellow, get thee home, provide some carts   105
And bring away the armour that is there.

[Exit Servingman.]

Gentlemen, will you go muster men? If I
Know how or which way to order these affairs,
Thus thrust disorderly into my hands,
Never believe me. Both are my kinsmen.   110
Th' one is my sovereign, whom both my oath
And duty bids defend; t' other again
Is my kinsman, whom the King hath wrong'd,
Whom conscience and my kindred bids to right.

---

85 *your son* Aumerle, who had left to join Richard in Ireland.   86 *so* so be it.
100 *So . . . to it* provided that no disloyalty on my part had incited him to such
an act [K].   104 *sister* Although York is speaking to the queen, he is thinking
of the death of the Duchess of Gloucester, his sister (-in-law). Shakespeare wishes
to portray him as flustered.   109 *thrust disorderly* STEEVENS; Q¹: "disorderly
thrust."   118 *presently* without delay.   120 *uneven* in disorder.   120 *at six and*

Well, somewhat we must do. Come, cousin, I'll   115
Dispose of you.
Gentlemen, go muster up your men,
And meet me presently at Berkeley Castle.
I should to Plashy too,
But time will not permit. All is uneven,   120
And everything is left at six and seven.
                                    Exeunt Duke, Queen.

BUSHY.   The wind sits fair for news to go for Ireland,
          But none returns. For us to levy power
          Proportionable to the enemy
          Is all unpossible.   125

GREEN.   Besides, our nearness to the King in love
          Is near the hate of those love not the King.

BAGOT.   And that's the wavering commons; for their love
          Lies in their purses, and whoso empties them,
          By so much fills their hearts with deadly hate.   130

BUSHY.   Wherein the King stands generally condemn'd.

BAGOT.   If judgment lie in them, then so do we,
          Because we ever have been near the King.

GREEN.   Well, I will for refuge straight to Bristow Castle.
          The Earl of Wiltshire is already there.   135

BUSHY.   Thither will I with you; for little office
          The hateful commons will perform for us,
          Except like curs to tear us all to pieces.
          Will you go along with us?

BAGOT.   No; I will to Ireland to his Majesty.   140
          Farewell. If heart's presages be not vain,
          We three here part that ne'er shall meet again.

BUSHY.   That's as York thrives to beat back Bolingbroke.

---

seven in a state of utter confusion (a common expression, coming originally from
dicing).   126–7 *our nearness . . . King* the fact that we are close friends with
the King exposes us to the hatred of those who do not love him [K].   131 *Wherein*
on which grounds. *generally* universally.   132 *If judgment lie in them* if they
are to pass judgment on us.   136 *office* service.   137 *hateful* full of hatred.
143 *to beat* in beating.

GREEN.   Alas, poor Duke! The task he undertakes
          Is numb'ring sands and drinking oceans dry.   145
          Where one on his side fights, thousands will fly.

BAGOT.   Farewell at once — for once, for all, and ever.

BUSHY.   Well, we may meet again.

BAGOT.   I fear me, never.

                                        Exeunt.

◇◇◇◇◇◇◇◇◇◇◇◇◇◇◇◇◇◇

          SCENE III. [*The wilds in Gloucestershire.*]

          Enter [Bolingbroke] *the* Duke of Hereford, *and*
              Northumberland.

BOLING.   How far is it, my lord, to Berkeley now?

NORTH.   Believe me, noble lord,
          I am a stranger here in Gloucestershire.
          These high wild hills and rough uneven ways
          Draws out our miles and makes them wearisome;   5
          And yet your fair discourse hath been as sugar,
          Making the hard way sweet and delectable.
          But I bethink me what a weary way
          From Ravenspurgh to Cotshall will be found
          In Ross and Willoughby, wanting your company,   10
          Which, I protest, hath very much beguil'd
          The tediousness and process of my travel;
          But theirs is sweet'ned with the hope to have
          The present benefit which I possess;
          And hope to joy is little less in joy   15
          Than hope enjoy'd. By this the weary lords
          Shall make their way seem short, as mine hath done

II.III. 9 *Cotshall* the Cotswolds in Gloucestershire. The Q¹ spelling, here pre-
served, may reflect Shakespeare's pronunciation.   12 *tediousness and process* weary
course.   15–16 *hope . . . enjoy'd* hope to enjoy possession of anything is hardly less
joyful than actually to enjoy the possession of what one hoped for [K].   22
whencesoever from somewhere or other.   34 *power* troops.   42 *raw* inexperienced.

By sight of what I have, your noble company.

BOLING. Of much less value is my company
          Than your good words. But who comes here?   20

Enter Harry Percy.

NORTH. It is my son, young Harry Percy,
        Sent from my brother Worcester, whencesoever.
        Harry, how fares your uncle?

PERCY. I had thought, my lord, to have learn'd his health of you.

NORTH. Why, is he not with the Queen?   25

PERCY. No, my good lord; he hath forsook the court,
        Broken his staff of office, and dispers'd
        The household of the King.

NORTH.   What was his reason?
        He was not so resolv'd when last we spake together.

PERCY. Because your lordship was proclaimed traitor.   30
        But he, my lord, is gone to Ravenspurgh
        To offer service to the Duke of Hereford;
        And sent me over by Berkeley to discover
        What power the Duke of York had levied there;
        Then with directions to repair to Ravenspurgh.   35

NORTH. Have you forgot the Duke of Hereford, boy?

PERCY. No, my good lord, for that is not forgot
        Which ne'er I did remember. To my knowledge,
        I never in my life did look on him.

NORTH. Then learn to know him now. This is the Duke.   40

PERCY. My gracious lord, I tender you my service,
        Such as it is, being tender, raw, and young;
        Which elder days shall ripen and confirm
        To more approved service and desert.

---

young Hotspur was, in fact, about thirty-five years of age at this time (1399). He
had distinguished himself at the siege of Berwick in 1378. Shakespeare's representation of him as a youth in this play prepares for the rivalry between him and Prince
Hal [k]. This provides one of the important dramatic links between RICHARD II
and 1 HENRY IV.   43 *confirm* strengthen.   44 *approved* demonstrated.

BOLING.   I thank thee, gentle Percy; and be sure   45
          I count myself in nothing else so happy
          As in a soul rememb'ring my good friends;
          And, as my fortune ripens with thy love,
          It shall be still thy true love's recompense.
          My heart this covenant makes, my hand thus seals it.   50

NORTH.   How far is it to Berkeley? and what stir
          Keeps good old York there with his men of war?

PERCY.   There stands the castle by yon tuft of trees,
          Mann'd with three hundred men, as I have heard;
          And in it are the Lords of York, Berkeley, and Seymour,   55
          None else of name and noble estimate.

                    Enter Ross *and* Willoughby.

NORTH.   Here come the Lords of Ross and Willoughby,
          Bloody with spurring, fiery red with haste.

BOLING.   Welcome, my lords. I wot your love pursues
          A banish'd traitor. All my treasury   60
          Is yet but unfelt thanks, which, more enrich'd,
          Shall be your love and labour's recompense.

ROSS.   Your presence makes us rich, most noble lord.

WIL.   And far surmounts our labour to attain it.

BOLING.   Evermore thanks, the exchequer of the poor,   65
          Which, till my infant fortune comes to years,
          Stands for my bounty. But who comes here?

                    Enter Berkeley.

NORTH.   It is my Lord of Berkeley, as I guess.

BERK.   My Lord of Hereford, my message is to you.

BOLING.   My lord, my answer is — "to Lancaster";   70

---

49 *still* constantly.   56 *estimate* estimation, rank.   59 *wot* know.   60-2 *All my . . . recompense* all that I yet have with which to reward your love is thanks, which, being mere words, you cannot feel as anything substantial; but when my treasury is richer (when I have something substantial with which to reward you) my whole store shall be the recompense of your devoted service [K].   65 *thanks* F¹; Q¹: "thank's" (thank is).   67 *Stands for my bounty* must represent all that I can do in the way of generosity [K].   75 *rase* erase.   *title* with a possible pun on

And I am come to seek that name in England;
And I must find that title in your tongue
Before I make reply to aught you say.

BERK.   Mistake me not, my lord. 'Tis not my meaning
To rase one title of your honour out.   75
To you, my lord, I come (what lord you will)
From the most gracious Regent of this land,
The Duke of York, to know what pricks you on
To take advantage of the absent time
And fright our native peace with self-borne arms.   80

Enter York [*attended*].

BOLING.   I shall not need transport my words by you;
Here comes his Grace in person. My noble uncle!
[*Kneels.*]

YORK.   Show me thy humble heart, and not thy knee,
Whose duty is deceivable and false.

BOLING.   My gracious uncle!   85

YORK.   Tut, tut!
Grace me no grace, nor uncle me no uncle.
I am no traitor's uncle, and that word "grace"
In an ungracious mouth is but profane.
Why have those banish'd and forbidden legs   90
Dar'd once to touch a dust of England's ground?
But then more why? — why have they dar'd to march
So many miles upon her peaceful bosom,
Frighting her pale-fac'd villages with war
And ostentation of despised arms?   95
Com'st thou because the anointed King is hence?
Why, foolish boy, the King is left behind,
And in my loyal bosom lies his power.
Were I but now lord of such hot youth

"tittle."   76 *what lord you will* whatever title you choose to be called.   78 *pricks*
spurs, incites.   79 *absent time* time of the King's absence.   80 *self-borne* (a)
borne in one's own interest rather than that of the state (b) self-born [K], arising
among ourselves, an antonym of "foreign," indicating civil warfare.   84 *deceivable*
deceitful.   89 *ungracious* graceless.   91 *dust* grain of dust.   95 *ostentation* defiant display.   *despised* despicable.

As when brave Gaunt thy father and myself   100
Rescued the Black Prince, that young Mars of men,
From forth the ranks of many thousand French,
O, then how quickly should this arm of mine,
Now prisoner to the palsy, chastise thee
And minister correction to thy fault!   105

BOLING. My gracious uncle, let me know my fault;
On what condition stands it and wherein?

YORK. Even in condition of the worst degree,
In gross rebellion and detested treason.
Thou art a banish'd man; and here art come,   110
Before the expiration of thy time,
In braving arms against thy sovereign.

BOLING. As I was banish'd, I was banish'd Hereford;
But as I come, I come for Lancaster.
And, noble uncle, I beseech your Grace   115
Look on my wrongs with an indifferent eye.
You are my father, for methinks in you
I see old Gaunt alive. O, then, my father,
Will you permit that I shall stand condemn'd
A wandering vagabond, my rights and royalties   120
Pluck'd from my arms perforce, and given away
To upstart unthrifts? Wherefore was I born?
If that my cousin king be King in England,
It must be granted I am Duke of Lancaster.
You have a son, Aumerle, my noble cousin.   125
Had you first died, and he been thus trod down,
He should have found his uncle Gaunt a father
To rouse his wrongs and chase them to the bay.
I am denied to sue my livery here,
And yet my letters patents give me leave.   130

100–2 *As when . . . French* No such episode is recorded in history.   104 *palsy*
paralysis.   107 *condition* personal quality in me. *wherein* of what does it con-
sist.   108 *condition . . . degree* the worst of all possible conditions (circum-
stances). York quibbles on "condition."   109 *detested* detestable.   112 *braving*
defiant.   116 *indifferent* impartial.   120 *royalties* rights as a member of the
royal family.   122 *unthrifts* spendthrifts. *Wherefore . . . born* what purpose is
served by my birth and lineal succession.   123–4 *If . . . Lancaster* Bolingbroke's
argument is the same as that with which York (II.I. 195–9) had protested against
the seizure of Gaunt's property. *in* Q¹; F¹, K: "of."   126 *first* before him.   128

My father's goods are all distrain'd and sold;
And these, and all, are all amiss employ'd.
What would you have me do? I am a subject,
And I challenge law. Attorneys are denied me,
And therefore personally I lay my claim   135
To my inheritance of free descent.

NORTH. The noble Duke hath been too much abus'd.

ROSS. It stands your Grace upon to do him right.

WIL. Base men by his endowments are made great.

YORK. My lords of England, let me tell you this: 140
I have had feeling of my cousin's wrongs,
And labour'd all I could to do him right;
But in this kind to come, in braving arms,
Be his own carver and cut out his way
To find out right with wrong — it may not be;   145
And you that do abet him in this kind
Cherish rebellion and are rebels all.

NORTH. The noble Duke hath sworn his coming is
But for his own; and for the right of that
We all have strongly sworn to give him aid;   150
And let him never see joy that breaks that oath!

YORK. Well, well, I see the issue of these arms.
I cannot mend it, I must needs confess,
Because my power is weak and all ill left;
But if I could, by him that gave me life,   155
I would attach you all and make you stoop
Unto the sovereign mercy of the King;
But since I cannot, be it known to you
I do remain as neuter. So fare you well —

---

rouse rout from cover. The metaphor is drawn from hunting.   chase . . . bay
hunt them to their final stand.   129 sue my livery formally demand the delivery
of my lands.   130 letters patents royal grants.   131 distrain'd seized by writ.
132 amiss employ'd put to a bad use.   134 challenge law demand my legal rights.
136 my inheritance of that which I am heir to by.   138 It stands it is incumbent
upon.   139 endowments revenue from his lands.   146 kind course of action.
154 power army. ill left poorly equipped.   156 attach arrest.   159 neuter neu-
tral.

Unless you please to enter in the castle   160
And there repose you for this night.

BOLING. An offer, uncle, that we will accept;
But we must win your Grace to go with us
To Bristow Castle, which they say is held
By Bushy, Bagot, and their complices,   165
The caterpillars of the commonwealth,
Which I have sworn to weed and pluck away.

YORK.   It may be I will go with you; but yet I'll pause,
For I am loath to break our country's laws.
Nor friends nor foes, to me welcome you are.   170
Things past redress are now with me past care.   *Exeunt.*

◇◇◇◇◇◇◇◇◇◇◇◇◇◇◇◇

SCENE IV. [*A camp in Wales.*]

Enter Earl of Salisbury *and a* Welsh Captain.

WELSH. My Lord of Salisbury, we have stay'd ten days
And hardly kept our countrymen together,
And yet we hear no tidings from the King.
Therefore we will disperse ourselves. Farewell.

SAL.   Stay yet another day, thou trusty Welshman.   5
The King reposeth all his confidence in thee.

WELSH. 'Tis thought the King is dead. We will not stay.
The bay trees in our country are all wither'd,
And meteors fright the fixed stars of heaven;
The pale-fac'd moon looks bloody on the earth,   10
And lean-look'd prophets whisper fearful change;
Rich men look sad, and ruffians dance and leap —

---

163 *win* induce. York is being arrested politely by Bolingbroke.   164 *Bristow*
Bristol.   165 *complices* accomplices.   166 *caterpillars* the regular term for "para-
sites" or persons who enrich themselves at others' expense — especially for corrupt
officials [K].   170 *Nor . . . are* I welcome you as neutrals — neither friends nor
foes [K].
    II.IV. *Welsh Captain* This may possibly be Owen Glendower, who figures so

The one in fear to lose what they enjoy,
The other to enjoy by rage and war.
These signs forerun the death or fall of kings.   15
Farewell. Our countrymen are gone and fled,
As well assur'd Richard their king is dead.   *Exit.*

SAL.   Ah, Richard! with the eyes of heavy mind,
I see thy glory, like a shooting star,
Fall to the base earth from the firmament.   20
Thy sun sets weeping in the lowly West,
Witnessing storms to come, woe, and unrest;
Thy friends are fled to wait upon thy foes,
And crossly to thy good all fortune goes.   *Exit.*

largely in 1 HENRY IV.   2 *hardly* with difficulty.   8 *are all* Q¹, F¹; Q²⁻⁵, K: "all are."
9 *meteors . . . heaven* Meteors were traditional symbols of change and disorder,
the fixed stars of order and stability.   11 *lean-look'd* lean-visaged. The suggestion
is that they are wasted with anxiety [K].   *change* political upheaval.   13 *enjoy*
possess.   14 *to enjoy* in hope of gaining.   *rage* violence.   22 *Witnessing* sig-
nifying.   23 *wait upon* offer allegiance to.   24 *crossly* adversely.

Act Three

◇◇

SCENE I. [Bolingbroke's *camp at Bristol.*]

Enter Bolingbroke Duke of Hereford, York, Northumberland, Ross, Percy, Willoughby, *with* Bushy *and*
Green *prisoners.*

BOLING. Bring forth these men.
Bushy and Green, I will not vex your souls
(Since presently your souls must part your bodies)
With too much urging your pernicious lives,
For 'twere no charity; yet, to wash your blood   5
From off my hands, here in the view of men
I will unfold some causes of your deaths.
You have misled a prince, a royal king,
A happy gentleman in blood and lineaments,
By you unhappied and disfigured clean.   10
You have in manner with your sinful hours
Made a divorce betwixt his queen and him,
Broke the possession of a royal bed,
And stain'd the beauty of a fair queen's cheeks
With tears drawn from her eyes by your foul wrongs.   15

III.i. 3 *presently* immediately. *part* depart from.   4 *urging* emphasizing.   9
happy fortunate. *blood* noble descent.   10 *unhappied* rendered unfortunate.
disfigured made a hateful figure in his subjects' eyes. *clean* completely.   11 *in
manner* in a manner of speaking. *sinful hours* association with him in riotous
living [K].   12–13 *Made . . . bed* There is no historical basis for the assertion that
Bushy and Green had thus estranged the King and Queen, for the Queen was
but nine years of age in fact. Nor does it accord with relations between Richard
and his queen in the play. Holinshed, however, asserts that the King was unfaith-

50

Myself — a prince by fortune of my birth,
Near to the King in blood, and near in love
Till you did make him misinterpret me —
Have stoop'd my neck under your injuries
And sigh'd my English breath in foreign clouds,   20
Eating the bitter bread of banishment,
Whilst you have fed upon my signories,
Dispark'd my parks and fell'd my forest woods,
From my own windows torn my household coat,
Ras'd out my imprese, leaving me no sign,   25
Save men's opinions and my living blood,
To show the world I am a gentleman.
This and much more, much more than twice all this,
Condemns you to the death. See them delivered over
To execution and the hand of death.   30

BUSHY.   More welcome is the stroke of death to me
          Than Bolingbroke to England. Lords, farewell.

GREEN.   My comfort is that heaven will take our souls
          And plague injustice with the pains of hell.

BOLING.   My Lord Northumberland, see them dispatch'd.   35

                    [*Exeunt* Northumberland *and others,*
                        with the prisoners.]

          Uncle, you say the Queen is at your house.
          For God's sake, fairly let her be entreated.
          Tell her I send to her my kind commends;
          Take special care my greetings be delivered.

YORK.   A gentleman of mine I have dispatch'd   40
          With letters of your love to her at large.

---

ful to his wife [K]. *Broke* interrupted.   17 *Near* closely related.   19 *stoop'd my
neck* submitted without resistance.   20 *sigh'd . . . clouds* augmenting foreign
clouds with my breath, as well as sighing in foreign countries.   22 *signories* estates.   23 *Dispark'd* opened to unauthorized use.   24 *coat* coat of arms (displayed
in painted windows).   25 *Ras'd out* erased.   *imprese* an heraldic device or emblem, with a motto [K].   37 *entreated* treated.   38 *commends* regards.   41 *at
large* in full.

BOLING. Thanks, gentle uncle. Come, lords, away,
         To fight with Glendower and his complices.
         Awhile to work, and after holiday.   *Exeunt.*

◇◇◇◇◇◇◇◇◇◇◇◇◇◇

SCENE II.

[*The coast of Wales. A castle in view.*]

Drums. Flourish and Colours. Enter the King, Aumerle,
[*the* Bishop of] Carlisle, *and* Soldiers.

KING. Barkloughly Castle call they this at hand?

AUM.   Yea, my lord. How brooks your Grace the air
       After your late tossing on the breaking seas?

KING. Needs must I like it well. I weep for joy
       To stand upon my kingdom once again.   5
       Dear earth, I do salute thee with my hand,
       Though rebels wound thee with their horses' hoofs.
       As a long-parted mother with her child
       Plays fondly with her tears and smiles in meeting,
       So weeping, smiling, greet I thee, my earth,   10
       And do thee favours with my royal hands.
       Feed not thy sovereign's foe, my gentle earth,
       Nor with thy sweets comfort his ravenous sense;
       But let thy spiders that suck up thy venom,
       And heavy-gaited toads, lie in their way,   15
       Doing annoyance to the treacherous feet

---

43 *Glendower.* There is no historical evidence that Bolingbroke launched an ex-
pedition against Glendower in 1399. This may be a link between RICHARD II and
1 HENRY IV.   44 *after* afterwards.
    III.II. 1 *Barkloughly* the present-day Harlech castle on the coast of North Wales.
Shakespeare is following Holinshed's "Barclowlie," an error for "Hertlowlie," an
early form of "Harlech."   2 *brooks* endures, enjoys.   3 *late* recent.   8 *long-
parted mother* mother long parted from.   9 *Plays . . . smiles* dallies with both
tears and smiles — not yielding to the full sway of either [K]. *fondly* dotingly.
11 *do . . . hands* salute thee by touching.   13 *comfort* satisfy. *ravenous sense*
voracious appetite.   16 *annoyance* injury.   21 *double* forked. *mortal* deadly.
touch wound.   23 *Mock . . . conjuration* do not ridicule my adjuration (my
solemn appeal), as being addressed to the earth, which has no sense of hearing

Which with usurping steps do trample thee.
Yield stinging nettles to mine enemies;
And when they from thy bosom pluck a flower,
Guard it, I pray thee, with a lurking adder   20
Whose double tongue may with a mortal touch
Throw death upon thy sovereign's enemies.
Mock not my senseless conjuration, lords.
This earth shall have a feeling, and these stones
Prove armed soldiers ere her native king   25
Shall falter under foul rebellion's arms.

CAR.   Fear not, my lord. That Power that made you king
Hath power to keep you king in spite of all.
The means that heaven yields must be embrac'd,
And not neglected; else, if heaven would,   30
And we will not, heaven's offer we refuse,
The proffered means of succour and redress.

AUM.   He means, my lord, that we are too remiss,
Whilst Bolingbroke, through our security,
Grows strong and great in substance and in power.   35

KING.   Discomfortable cousin! know'st thou not
That when the searching eye of heaven is hid
Behind the globe, that lights the lower world,
Then thieves and robbers range abroad unseen
In murders and in outrage boldly here;   40
But when from under this terrestrial ball
He fires the proud tops of the Eastern pines
And darts his light through every guilty hole,
Then murders, treasons, and detested sins,

---

or feeling [K].   25 *native* legitimate (not native-born, since Richard was born at
Bordeaux).   29-32 *The means . . . redress* These lines were omitted from F¹,
possibly, as has been suggested, because no sense could be made of them, since the
passage as it appears in the quartos is corrupt. POPE's emendations are followed
here.   29 *heaven yields* POPE; QQ: "heauens yeeld."   30 *if* POPE; omitted in QQ.
32 *succour* POPE QQ: "succours."   34 *security,* negligence, overconfidence.   36
Discomfortable discouraging.   37-8 *when . . . world* when the sun is hidden
from view while it is lighting the lower half of the globe.   38 *that* the sun. The
earth in the Ptolemaic system of astronomy was conceived as the centre of the
universe about which the sun revolved.   40 *boldly* Q¹: "bouldy"; Q²⁻⁵, F¹: "bloody"
is followed by some editors.   43 *guilty hole* hiding place of the guilty.   44 *detested* detestable.

The cloak of night being pluck'd from off their backs,   45
Stand bare and naked, trembling at themselves?
So when this thief, this traitor Bolingbroke,
Who all this while hath revell'd in the night
Whilst we were wand'ring with the Antipodes,
Shall see us rising in our throne, the East,   50
His treasons will sit blushing in his face,
Not able to endure the sight of day,
But self-affrighted tremble at his sin.
Not all the water in the rough rude sea
Can wash the balm off from an anointed king.   55
The breath of worldly men cannot depose
The deputy elected by the Lord.
For every man that Bolingbroke hath press'd
To lift shrewd steel against our golden crown,
God for his Richard hath in heavenly pay   60
A glorious angel. Then, if angels fight,
Weak men must fall; for heaven still guards the right.

Enter Salisbury.

Welcome, my lord. How far off lies your power?

SAL.   Nor near nor farther off, my gracious lord,
Than this weak arm. Discomfort guides my tongue   65
And bids me speak of nothing but despair.
One day too late, I fear me, noble lord,
Hath clouded all thy happy days on earth.
O, call back yesterday, bid time return,
And thou shalt have twelve thousand fighting men!   70
To-day, to-day, unhappy day too late,
O'erthrows thy joys, friends, fortune, and thy state;
For all the Welshmen, hearing thou wert dead,
Are gone to Bolingbroke, dispers'd, and fled.

---

49 *we* I, the King — the sun of this realm of England. Richard feels sure that his
return from Ireland will put an immediate end to Bolingbroke's rebellion. The
Folio omits this verse [K]. *Antipodes* people believed to live on the opposite side
of the earth.   55 *balm* consecrated oil used in the coronation ceremony.   56
worldly mortal, of this world.   58 *press'd* impressed, drafted.   59 *shrewd* harm-
ful, accursed.   62 *still* always.   63 *power* army.   64 *near* nearer.   65 *Discomfort*

AUM.	Comfort, my liege. Why looks your Grace so pale? 75

KING.   But now the blood of twenty thousand men
    Did triumph in my face, and they are fled;
And, till so much blood thither come again,
    Have I not reason to look pale and dead?
All souls that will be safe, fly from my side;   80
For time hath set a blot upon my pride.

AUM.   Comfort, my liege. Remember who you are.

KING.   I had forgot myself. Am I not King?
Awake, thou coward majesty! thou sleepest.
Is not the King's name twenty thousand names?   85
Arm, arm, my name! A puny subject strikes
At thy great glory. Look not to the ground,
Ye favourites of a king. Are we not high?
High be our thoughts. I know my uncle York
Hath power enough to serve our turn. But who comes
    here?   90

Enter Scroop.

SCROOP.   More health and happiness betide my liege
Than can my care-tun'd tongue deliver him!

KING.   Mine ear is open and my heart prepar'd.
The worst is worldly loss thou canst unfold.
Say, is my kingdom lost? Why, 'twas my care;   95
And what loss is it to be rid of care?
Strives Bolingbroke to be as great as we?
Greater he shall not be; if he serve God,
We'll serve him too, and be his fellow so.
Revolt our subjects? That we cannot mend;   100
They break their faith to God as well as us.
Cry woe, destruction, ruin, and decay:
The worst is death, and death will have his day.

---

helplessness.   72 *state* royal authority.   75 *Comfort* take comfort.   77 *tri-umph* glow triumphantly.   90 *power* troops.   91 *Scroop* Sir Stephan Scroope, brother of Sir William Scroope, Earl of Wiltshire.   92 *care-tun'd* tuned to sounds of sorrow.   *deliver* report to.   94 *The worst . . . unfold* the worst which thou canst disclose is loss of worldly possessions [K].   95 *care* source of trouble.   102 *Cry* proclaim.

SCROOP. Glad am I that your Highness is so arm'd
To bear the tidings of calamity.   105
Like an unseasonable stormy day
Which makes the silver rivers drown their shores
As if the world were all dissolv'd to tears,
So high above his limits swells the rage
Of Bolingbroke, covering your fearful land   110
With hard bright steel, and hearts harder than steel.
White-beards have arm'd their thin and hairless scalps
Against thy majesty. Boys with women's voices
Strive to speak big, and clap their female joints
In stiff unwieldy arms against thy crown.   115
Thy very beadsmen learn to bend their bows
Of double-fatal yew against thy state.
Yea, distaff-women manage rusty bills
Against thy seat. Both young and old rebel,
And all goes worse than I have power to tell.   120

KING. Too well, too well thou tell'st a tale so ill.
Where is the Earl of Wiltshire? Where is Bagot?
What is become of Bushy? Where is Green?
That they have let the dangerous enemy
Measure our confines with such peaceful steps?   125
If we prevail, their heads shall pay for it.
I warrant they have made peace with Bolingbroke.

SCROOP. Peace have they made with him indeed, my lord.

KING. O villains, vipers, damn'd without redemption!
Dogs easily won to fawn on any man!   130
Snakes in my heart-blood warm'd that sting my heart!

107 *drown* overflow.   109 *his* its.   *limits* banks.   110 *fearful* terrified.   112 *arm'd* with helmets.   *thin* scanty-haired.   114 *clap* thrust hurriedly.   *female* weak as women's.   115 *In* into.   116 *beadsmen* aged pensioners, whose duty was to pray for their benefactors [K].   117 *double-fatal* because its leaves and berries are poisonous and its wood is used for deadly weapons (bows) [K]. *yew* Q¹⁻²: "ewe"; Q³⁻⁵: "woe"; F¹: "Eugh."   *state* royal majesty.   118 *distaff-women* women, who should wield nothing more dangerous than the distaff — a staff used in spinning, and regarded (like the broomstick in modern times) as the characteristic weapon of women [K].   *manage* wield.   *bills* halberds, pikes.   119 *seat* throne.   125 *Measure* traverse.   *confines* territories.   *peaceful* unopposed.   134 *spotted* stained with treason.   *offence* F¹; omitted in QQ.   135 *changing his property* when it changes from its essential quality.   138 *with hands* with hands raised in submis-

Three Judases, each one thrice worse than Judas!
Would they make peace? Terrible hell make war
Upon their spotted souls for this offence!

SCROOP. Sweet love, I see, changing his property,   135
Turns to the sourest and most deadly hate.
Again uncurse their souls. Their peace is made
With heads, and not with hands. Those whom you curse
Have felt the worst of death's destroying wound
And lie full low, grav'd in the hollow ground.   140

AUM. Is Bushy, Green, and the Earl of Wiltshire dead?

SCROOP. Ay, all of them at Bristow lost their heads.

AUM. Where is the Duke my father with his power?

KING. No matter where. Of comfort no man speak!
Let's talk of graves, of worms, and epitaphs,   145
Make dust our paper, and with rainy eyes
Write sorrow on the bosom of the earth.
Let's choose executors and talk of wills.
And yet not so — for what can we bequeath,
Save our deposed bodies to the ground?   150
Our lands, our lives, and all are Bolingbroke's,
And nothing can we call our own but death
And that small model of the barren earth
Which serves as paste and cover to our bones.
For God's sake let us sit upon the ground   155
And tell sad stories of the death of kings!
How some have been depos'd, some slain in war,
Some haunted by the ghosts they have depos'd,
Some poisoned by their wives, some sleeping kill'd —

---

sion.   140 grav'd buried.   150 deposed bodies Richard already sees himself as
a deposed king. It is significant that the scene's first mention of deposition should
come from him.   153 small model . . . earth (a) that small quantity of barren
earth which outlines the shape of our body as we lie in the grave [K] (b) the
human flesh, being composed of the same physical elements as the earth, and
therefore conceived of as a small representation of it, which covers our bones.
154 paste and cover The metaphor is from a pie.   156 sad stories Many such
tragic tales occur in THE MIRROR FOR MAGISTRATES (1559–1587), which was a very
popular book in Shakespeare's time. Its predecessors were Boccaccio's DE CASIBUS
ILLUSTRIUM VIRORUM and Lydgate's FALLS OF PRINCES [K].   158 ghosts of murdered kings.

All murdered; for within the hollow crown   160
That rounds the mortal temples of a king
Keeps Death his court; and there the antic sits,
Scoffing his state and grinning at his pomp;
Allowing him a breath, a little scene,
To monarchize, be fear'd, and kill with looks;   165
Infusing him with self and vain conceit,
As if this flesh which walls about our life
Were brass impregnable; and humour'd thus,
Comes at the last, and with a little pin
Bores through his castle wall, and farewell king!   170
Cover your heads, and mock not flesh and blood
With solemn reverence. Throw away respect,
Tradition, form, and ceremonious duty;
For you have but mistook me all this while.
I live with bread like you, feel want, taste grief,   175
Need friends. Subjected thus,
How can you say to me I am a king?

CAR.   My lord, wise men ne'er sit and wail their woes,
But presently prevent the ways to wail.
To fear the foe, since fear oppresseth strength,   180
Gives, in your weakness, strength unto your foe,
And so your follies fight against yourself.
Fear, and be slain — no worse can come to fight;
And fight and die is death destroying death,
Where fearing dying pays death servile breath.   185

AUM.   My father hath a power. Inquire of him,

160–2 *for within . . . court* For grotesque figures of Death in skeleton form see
the old collection known as THE DANCE OF DEATH [K].   162 *antic* grotesque. Death
was traditionally portrayed as grinning at the vain pretensions of mankind.   163
Scoffing his state ridiculing his royal splendour.   *pomp* magnificence.   164 *little*
scene short time — as in a play [K].   165 *monarchize* play the part of a king.
166 *self and vain conceit* empty self-deception, the belief that he is immortal.
168 *humour'd thus* (a) when he (the king) has been thus indulged in his delusion
[K] (b) when Death has amused himself in this way. Either meaning or both may
have been intended.   169 *Comes* i.e. Death.   170 *castle wall* the wall of his
mortal body [K].   176 *Subjected thus* (a) since I am reduced to the condition of a
subject [K] (b) subject as I am to these universal conditions.   179 *presently*

And learn to make a body of a limb.

KING. Thou chid'st me well. Proud Bolingbroke, I come
To change blows with thee for our day of doom.
This ague fit of fear is overblown.   190
An easy task it is to win our own.
Say, Scroop, where lies our uncle with his power?
Speak sweetly, man, although thy looks be sour.

SCROOP. Men judge by the complexion of the sky
The state and inclination of the day;   195
So may you by my dull and heavy eye:
My tongue hath but a heavier tale to say.
I play the torturer, by small and small
To lengthen out the worst that must be spoken.
Your uncle York is join'd with Bolingbroke,   200
And all your Northern castles yielded up,
And all your Southern gentlemen in arms
Upon his party.

KING.   Thou hast said enough.
[To Aumerle] Beshrew thee, cousin, which didst lead me
forth
Of that sweet way I was in to despair!   205
What say you now? What comfort have we now?
By heaven, I'll hate him everlastingly
That bids me be of comfort any more.
Go to Flint Castle. There I'll pine away;
A king, woe's slave, shall kingly woe obey.   210
That power I have, discharge; and let them go

promptly. *prevent . . . wail* cut off in advance the courses of action that lead
one to lament [K].   180 *oppresseth* destroys the effect of.   183 *to fight* if one
fights.   184 *And fight . . . death* to die fighting is to destroy death by means of
death.   185 *Where . . . breath* whereas to die in fear is to yield cowardly and
slavish obedience to death's commands [K].   186 *of* about.   187 *make . . . limb*
to make a whole army out of a single troop—by mustering additional forces [K].
189 *change* exchange. *for . . . doom* to determine which of us shall be doomed
by defeat [K].   195 *state . . . day* condition of the weather.   197 *heavier*
gloomier.   198 *torturer* The allusion is to the torture of the rack [K]. *small and
small* little by little.   199 *to lengthen* in lengthening.   203 *Upon his party* on
his side.   204 *Beshrew* confound. *forth* out.

To ear the land that hath some hope to grow,
For I have none. Let no man speak again
To alter this, for counsel is but vain.

AUM.   My liege, one word.

KING.   He does me double wrong   215
That wounds me with the flatteries of his tongue.
Discharge my followers. Let them hence away,
From Richard's night to Bolingbroke's fair day.

                                        Exeunt.

◇◇◇◇◇◇◇◇◇◇◇◇◇◇◇

SCENE III. [*Wales. Before Flint Castle.*]

Enter, with Drum *and* Colours, Bolingbroke, York,
    Northumberland, Attendants, [*and* Soldiers].

BOLING.   So that by this intelligence we learn
The Welshmen are dispers'd, and Salisbury
Is gone to meet the King, who lately landed
With some few private friends upon this coast.

NORTH.   The news is very fair and good, my lord.   5
Richard not far from hence hath hid his head.

YORK.   It would beseem the Lord Northumberland
To say 'King Richard.' Alack the heavy day
When such a sacred king should hide his head!

NORTH.   Your Grace mistakes. Only to be brief,   10
Left I his title out.

YORK.   The time hath been,
Would you have been so brief with him, he would
Have been so brief with you to shorten you,
For taking so the head, your whole head's length.

---

212 *To ear . . . grow* to plough the soil that has some prospect of a harvest —
Bolingbroke's cause which is so much more promising than mine [K].   215
wrong injury.

    III.III. 1 *intelligence* information.   15 *Mistake* misinterpret Northumberland's
language.   17 *mistake* take that to which you have no claim [K]. Since there is

BOLING.	Mistake not, uncle, further than you should. 15
YORK.	Take not, good cousin, further than you should,
	Lest you mistake. The heavens are over our heads.
BOLING.	I know it, uncle, and oppose not myself
	Against their will. But who comes here?

Enter Percy.

	Welcome, Harry. What, will not this castle yield? 20
PERCY.	The castle royally is mann'd, my lord,
	Against thy entrance.
BOLING.	Royally?
	Why, it contains no king?
PERCY.	Yes, my good lord,
	It doth contain a king. King Richard lies 25
	Within the limits of yon lime and stone;
	And with him are the Lord Aumerle, Lord Salisbury,
	Sir Stephen Scroop, besides a clergyman
	Of holy reverence — who, I cannot learn.
NORTH.	O, belike it is the Bishop of Carlisle. 30
BOLING.	Noble lords,
	Go to the rude ribs of that ancient castle;
	Through brazen trumpet send the breath of parley
	Into his ruin'd ears, and thus deliver:
	Henry Bolingbroke 35
	On both his knees doth kiss King Richard's hand
	And sends allegiance and true faith of heart
	To his most royal person; hither come
	Even at his feet to lay my arms and power,
	Provided that my banishment repeal'd 40
	And lands restor'd again be freely granted.
	If not, I'll use the advantage of my power,

---

no punctuation after the word in QQ and F¹, some editors take "mistake" to mean
"fail to recognize that." But Q¹ punctuation is often scanty.   30 *belike* probably.
32 *rude ribs* rough walls.   33 *brazen* (a) bronze (b) loud blaring.   34 *ruin'd ears*
(a) ruined casements or loopholes of the castle, or (b) Richard's ears, ruined by
the sounds of flattery.   40 *repeal'd* revoked.

And lay the summer's dust with show'rs of blood
Rain'd from the wounds of slaughtered Englishmen;
The which, how far off from the mind of Bolingbroke   45
It is, such crimson tempest should bedrench
The fresh green lap of fair King Richard's land,
My stooping duty tenderly shall show.
Go signify as much, while here we march
Upon the grassy carpet of this plain.   50
Let's march without the noise of threat'ning drum,
That from this castle's tattered battlements
Our fair appointments may be well perus'd.
Methinks King Richard and myself should meet
With no less terror than the elements   55
Of fire and water when their thund'ring shock
At meeting tears the cloudy cheeks of heaven.
Be he the fire, I'll be the yielding water;
The rage be his, whilst on the earth I rain
My waters — on the earth, and not on him.   60
March on, and mark King Richard how he looks.

> *Parle without, and answer within;*
> *then a flourish. Enter, on the walls,*
> [King] Richard, [*the* Bishop of] Car-
> lisle, Aumerle, Scroop, Salisbury.

See, see, King Richard doth himself appear,
As doth the blushing discontented sun
From out the fiery portal of the East
When he perceives the envious clouds are bent   65
To dim his glory and to stain the track
Of his bright passage to the Occident.

YORK.   Yet looks he like a king. Behold, his eye,

---

48 *stooping duty* reverential obeisance. *tenderly* with affection. 52 *tattered* ruined. Bolingbroke is implying that the castle may easily be taken. 53 *fair appointments* handsome equipment. *perus'd* scanned. 55–7 *the elements . . . heaven* One old scientific explanation of thunder was that it is caused by a clash between the contrary elements of fire and water. A fiery vapour bursts forth from a water cloud in which it is confined [K]. 63 *blushing discontented sun* A red sun in the morning is said to be a sign of a stormy day [K]. 65 *he* the sun. *envious* hostile. 68 *he* Richard. 69–70 *lightens . . . majesty* flashes with authoritative majesty [K]. 71 *show* sight. 72–3 *stood . . . knee* stood silent wait-

As bright as is the eagle's, lightens forth
Controlling majesty. Alack, alack, for woe,   70
That any harm should stain so fair a show!

KING.   [to Northumberland] We are amaz'd; and thus long
              have we stood
         To watch the fearful bending of thy knee,
         Because we thought ourself thy lawful king.
         And if we be, how dare thy joints forget   75
         To pay their awful duty to our presence?
         If we be not, show us the hand of God
         That hath dismiss'd us from our stewardship;
         For well we know no hand of blood and bone
         Can gripe the sacred handle of our sceptre,   80
         Unless he do profane, steal, or usurp.
         And though you think that all, as you have done,
         Have torn their souls by turning them from us
         And we are barren and bereft of friends,
         Yet know, my master, God omnipotent,   85
         Is mustering in his clouds on our behalf
         Armies of pestilence, and they shall strike
         Your children yet unborn and unbegot
         That lift your vassal hands against my head
         And threat the glory of my precious crown.   90
         Tell Bolingbroke, for yon methinks he stands,
         That every stride he makes upon my land
         Is dangerous treason. He is come to open
         The purple testament of bleeding war.
         But ere the crown he looks for live in peace,   95
         Ten thousand bloody crowns of mothers' sons
         Shall ill become the flower of England's face,

---

ing to see thee bend thy knee in reverence [K].   76 *awful duty* reverential homage.   80 *gripe* seize.   81 *Unless he do profane* without committing sacrilege.
83 *torn their souls* torn their souls asunder. Thus their allegiance was no longer
wholehearted: they had given half their souls to Richard, and now the other
half to Bolingbroke [K].   89 *vassal* subject.   93 *dangerous* dangerous not only
to himself but to posterity [K].   93-4 *open . . . war* carry out the provisions of
the bloody (purple) will of bloody war.   96 *crowns* heads.   97 *flower . . . face*
the flowered surface of the land.

Change the complexion of her maid-pale peace
To scarlet indignation, and bedew
Her pastures' grass with faithful English blood.   100

NORTH. The King of Heaven forbid our lord the King
Should so with civil and uncivil arms
Be rush'd upon! Thy thrice-noble cousin
Harry Bolingbroke doth humbly kiss thy hand;
And by the honourable tomb he swears   105
That stands upon your royal grandsire's bones,
And by the royalties of both your bloods
(Currents that spring from one most gracious head),
And by the buried hand of warlike Gaunt,
And by the worth and honour of himself,   110
Comprising all that may be sworn or said,
His coming hither hath no further scope
Than for his lineal royalties, and to beg
Enfranchisement immediate on his knees;
Which on thy royal party granted once,   115
His glittering arms he will commend to rust,
His barbed steeds to stables, and his heart
To faithful service of your Majesty.
This swears he, as he is a prince, is just;
And as I am a gentleman, I credit him.   120

KING. Northumberland, say thus the King returns:
His noble cousin is right welcome hither;
And all the number of his fair demands
Shall be accomplish'd without contradiction.
With all the gracious utterance thou hast   125
Speak to his gentle hearing kind commends.
[*To* Aumerle] We do debase ourselves, cousin, do we not,

---

100 *pastures'* QQ, F¹: "pastors."   102 *civil* borne by Englishmen against Englishmen.
uncivil barbarous.   106 *royal grandsire's* Edward III's. The tomb is in Westminster Abbey.   107 *bloods* lineages.   108 *gracious* noble. *head* fountainhead,
source.   111 *Comprising . . . said* which includes every oath that can be sworn.
112 *scope* aim.   113 *lineal royalties* royal birthrights.   114 *Enfranchisement* release from banishment.   115 *party* part.   116 *commend* hand over.   117 *barbed*
armoured (with barbs, protective coverings for a horse's chest and flanks).   119
a prince, is just F¹; Q¹: "princesse just."   120 *credit* believe.   121 *returns* sends
back in reply.   124 *accomplish'd* granted.   125-6 *With . . . commends* use your

To look so poorly and to speak so fair?
Shall we call back Northumberland and send
Defiance to the traitor, and so die?   130

AUM.   No, good my lord. Let's fight with gentle words
Till time lend friends, and friends their helpful swords.

KING.   O God, O God! that e'er this tongue of mine
That laid the sentence of dread banishment
On yon proud man, should take it off again   135
With words of sooth! O that I were as great
As is my grief, or lesser than my name!
Or that I could forget what I have been!
Or not remember what I must be now!
Swell'st thou, proud heart? I'll give thee scope to beat,   140
Since foes have scope to beat both thee and me.

AUM.   Northumberland comes back from Bolingbroke.

KING.   What must the King do now? Must he submit?
The King shall do it. Must he be depos'd?
The King shall be contented. Must he lose   145
The name of king? A God's name, let it go!
I'll give my jewels for a set of beads,
My gorgeous palace for a hermitage,
My gay apparel for an almsman's gown,
My figur'd goblets for a dish of wood,   150
My sceptre for a palmer's walking staff,
My subjects for a pair of carved saints,
And my large kingdom for a little grave,
A little little grave, an obscure grave;
Or I'll be buried in the king's highway,   155
Some way of common trade, where subjects' feet

---

utmost courtesy in tone and words in giving him my kind regards, so that he may
receive your message with favour [K].   136 *sooth* flattery, appeasement.   137 *name*
title, King.   139 *must be now* a commoner. Richard recognizes that in sub-
mitting to the demands of a subject he can no longer be an absolute king.   140
scope permission.   146 *A* in.   147 *set of beads* rosary.   150 *figur'd* ornamented
with patterns.   151 *palmer* Palmers were pilgrims who had made a vow to
wander from shrine to shrine for life or for a term of years. They were originally
so called from carrying a palm branch as evidence that they had visited the Holy
Sepulchre at Jerusalem [K].   156 *trade* traffic.

May hourly trample on their sovereign's head;
For on my heart they tread now whilst I live,
And buried once, why not upon my head?
Aumerle, thou weep'st, my tender-hearted cousin!　160
We'll make foul weather with despised tears;
Our sighs and they shall lodge the summer corn
And make a dearth in this revolting land.
Or shall we play the wantons with our woes
And make some pretty match with shedding tears?　165
As thus — to drop them still upon one place
Till they have fretted us a pair of graves
Within the earth; and therein laid — there lies
Two kinsmen digg'd their graves with weeping eyes.
Would not this ill do well? Well, well, I see　170
I talk but idly, and you laugh at me.
Most mighty prince, my Lord Northumberland,
What says King Bolingbroke? Will his Majesty
Give Richard leave to live till Richard die?
You make a leg, and Bolingbroke says ay.　175

NORTH.　My lord, in the base court he doth attend
To speak with you, may it please you to come down.

KING.　Down, down I come, like glist'ring Phaëton,
Wanting the manage of unruly jades.
In the base court? Base court, where kings grow base,　180
To come at traitors' calls and do them grace!
In the base court? Come down? Down court! down king!
For night owls shriek where mounting larks should sing.
　　　　　　　　　　　　[*Exeunt from above.*]

BOLING.　What says his Majesty?

---

162 *lodge* beat down.　*corn* grain.　163 *dearth* famine.　164–5 *play* . . . *tears* sport with our own sorrows and play some clever game by shedding tears [K]. 166 *still* always, in a continuing stream.　167 *fretted* eaten away.　*us* for us. 171 *idly* foolishly. In the next sentence Richard changes to a satirical parody of the style of a formal petition [K].　175 *leg* curtsy.　176 *base court* lower or outer courtyard of the castle.　178 *Phaëton* the son of Apollo who borrowed his father's sun-chariot and, being too weak to control it, came too close to the earth. Zeus destroyed him with a thunderbolt to prevent the world's destruction.　179 *wanting* lacking.　*manage* ability to control.　*jades* horses (a contemptuous term).

NORTH.   Sorrow and grief of heart
          Makes him speak fondly, like a frantic man.   185
          Yet he is come.

                [*Enter* King Richard *attended, below.*]

BOLING.   Stand all apart
          And show fair duty to his Majesty.
                            He kneels down.
          My gracious lord —

KING.   Fair cousin, you debase your princely knee   190
          To make the base earth proud with kissing it.
          Me rather had my heart might feel your love
          Than my unpleas'd eye see your courtesy.
          Up, cousin, up! Your heart is up, I know,
          Thus high at least [*touches his own head*] although your
              knee be low.   195

BOLING.   [*rises*] My gracious lord, I come but for mine own.

KING.   Your own is yours, and I am yours, and all.

BOLING.   So far be mine, my most redoubted lord,
          As my true service shall deserve your love.

KING.   Well you deserve. They well deserve to have   200
          That know the strong'st and surest way to get.
          Uncle, give me your hands. Nay, dry your eyes.
          Tears show their love, but want their remedies.
          Cousin, I am too young to be your father,
          Though you are old enough to be my heir.   205
          What you will have, I'll give, and willing too;

---

181 *grace* honour.   183 *night owls shriek* an omen of disaster or death [K].
185 *fondly* foolishly. *frantic* raving mad.   192 *Me rather had* I had rather.
198 *mine* my friend. *redoubted* held in awe.   200 *Well you deserve* The
King plays with the word. He seems to mean "deserve my love," but the next sentence shows his real meaning [K].   202 *Uncle* York. *hands* QQ; F¹, K: "hand."
203 *Tears . . . remedies* Tears are personified: they reveal their love for the person for whom they are shed, but they lack the power to remedy the misfortunes
with which they show sympathy [K].   204–5 *too young . . . heir* As a matter of
fact, the King and Bolingbroke were of the same age, thirty-three years.

For do we must what force will have us do.
Set on towards London. Cousin, is it so?

BOLING. Yea, my good lord.

KING.   Then I must not say no.

Flourish. Exeunt.

◇◇◇◇◇◇◇◇◇◇◇◇◇◇◇◇

SCENE IV.

[Langley. The Duke of York's garden.]

Enter the Queen with two Ladies, her Attendants.

QUEEN. What sport shall we devise here in this garden
To drive away the heavy thought of care?

LADY. Madam, we'll play at bowls.

QUEEN. 'Twill make me think the world is full of rubs
And that my fortune runs against the bias.   5

LADY. Madam, we'll dance.

QUEEN. My legs can keep no measure in delight
When my poor heart no measure keeps in grief.
Therefore no dancing, girl; some other sport.

LADY. Madam, we'll tell tales.   10

QUEEN. Of sorrow or of joy?

LADY.   Of either, madam.

QUEEN. Of neither, girl;
For if of joy, being altogether wanting,
It doth remember me the more of sorrow;

III.IV. 4 *rubs* impediments in the game of bowls.   5 *bias* curving course of the
bowling ball. Specifically the bias is the leaden weight in the ball which causes
it to curve.   7 *measure* figure in dancing.   8 *measure* moderation, limit.   11
joy ROWE; QQ, F¹: "griefe."   14 *remember* remind.   15 *had* by me.   18 *boots*
avails.   22–3 *And . . . thee* I would sing (for joy) if weeping were capable of
ending my sorrows, and then I would never ask you to weep for me.   26 *wretched-*
ness . . . pins my grief wagered against a trifle. *pins* F¹; QQ: "pines."   27 *state*

Or if of grief, being altogether had,   15
It adds more sorrow to my want of joy;
For what I have I need not to repeat,
And what I want it boots not to complain.

LADY.   Madam, I'll sing.

QUEEN.   'Tis well that thou hast cause;
But thou shouldst please me better, wouldst thou weep.   20

LADY.   I could weep, madam, would it do you good.

QUEEN.   And I could sing, would weeping do me good,
And never borrow any tear of thee.

Enter a Gardener *and two* Servants.

But stay, here come the gardeners.
Let's step into the shadow of these trees.   25
My wretchedness unto a row of pins,
They will talk of state, for every one doth so
Against a change: woe is forerun with woe.

[Queen *and* Ladies *step aside.*]

GARD.   Go bind thou up yon dangling apricocks,
Which, like unruly children, make their sire   30
Stoop with oppression of their prodigal weight.
Give some supportance to the bending twigs.
Go thou and, like an executioner,
Cut off the heads of too fast growing sprays
That look too lofty in our commonwealth.   35
All must be even in our government.
You thus employ'd, I will go root away
The noisome weeds which without profit suck
The soil's fertility from wholesome flowers.

politics.   28 *Against a change* on the eve of any change in the political situation.
The Queen is thinking of a change for the worse, as the next sentence shows.
Gloomy forebodings precede the woeful change that is imminent [K].   29 *yon*
Q^{2-5}; F^1: "yond"; Q^1: "young" is preferred by some editors.   31 *prodigal* excessive.
33 *thou* the other servant.   35 *commonwealth* The analogy between garden and
state is common both in classical and medieval literature.   36 *even* equal.   38
noisome noxious. *without profit* doing no good.

MAN.   Why should we, in the compass of a pale,   40
         Keep law and form and due proportion,
         Showing, as in a model, our firm estate,
         When our sea-walled garden, the whole land,
         Is full of weeds, her fairest flowers chok'd up,
         Her fruit trees all unprun'd, her hedges ruin'd,   45
         Her knots disordered, and her wholesome herbs
         Swarming with caterpillars?

GARD.   Hold thy peace.
         He that hath suffer'd this disordered spring
         Hath now himself met with the fall of leaf.
         The weeds which his broad-spreading leaves did shelter,   50
         That seem'd in eating him to hold him up,
         Are pluck'd up root and all by Bolingbroke —
         I mean the Earl of Wiltshire, Bushy, Green.

MAN.   What, are they dead?

GARD.   They are; and Bolingbroke
         Hath seiz'd the wasteful King. O, what pity is it   55
         That he had not so trimm'd and dress'd his land
         As we this garden! We at time of year
         Do wound the bark, the skin of our fruit trees,
         Lest, being over-proud in sap and blood,
         With too much riches it confound itself.   60
         Had he done so to great and growing men,
         They might have liv'd to bear, and he to taste
         Their fruits of duty. Superfluous branches
         We lop away, that bearing boughs may live.
         Had he done so, himself had borne the crown,
         Which waste of idle hours hath quite thrown down.   66

MAN.   What, think you the King shall be depos'd?

---

40 *compass* limits. *pale* enclosed garden.   42 *Showing . . . estate* thus showing
our well-established organization, as if by way of model or pattern for the government of a kingdom [K].   46 *knots* patterned flower-beds.   48 *suffer'd* permitted.
49 *fall of leaf* autumn.   51 *in* while.   57 *We* CAPELL; not in QQ, F¹. *time of year*
proper season.   59 *over-proud in* swollen with.   60 *confound* destroy.   62–3
They might . . . duty they might have lived to bear fruit, and he, in his lifetime,
might have tasted that fruit — their dutiful service [K].   66 *idle hours* (a) idle-
ness (b) folly.   68 *Depress'd* put down, humbled.   69 *'Tis doubt* it is feared.

GARD.   Depress'd he is already, and depos'd
'Tis doubt he will be. Letters came last night
To a dear friend of the good Duke of York's   70
That tell black tidings.

QUEEN.   O, I am press'd to death through want of speaking!

[*Comes forward.*]

Thou old Adam's likeness, set to dress this garden,
How dares thy harsh rude tongue sound this unpleasing
        news?
What Eve, what serpent, hath suggested thee   75
To make a second fall of cursed man?
Why dost thou say King Richard is depos'd?
Dar'st thou, thou little better thing than earth,
Divine his downfall? Say, where, when, and how
Cam'st thou by this ill tidings? Speak, thou wretch!   80

GARD.   Pardon me, madam. Little joy have I
To breathe this news; yet what I say is true.
King Richard, he is in the mighty hold
Of Bolingbroke. Their fortunes both are weigh'd.
In your lord's scale is nothing but himself,   85
And some few vanities that make him light;
But in the balance of great Bolingbroke,
Besides himself, are all the English peers,
And with that odds he weighs King Richard down.
Post you to London, and you will find it so.   90
I speak no more than every one doth know.

QUEEN.   Nimble mischance, that art so light of foot,
Doth not thy embassage belong to me,

---

72 *press'd* . . . *speaking* Pressing to death by laying heavy weights upon the body
"la peine forte et dure" was the regular English penalty for "standing mute,"
refusing to plead guilty or not guilty [K].   73 *Adam* the first gardener. *set* ap-
pointed. *dress* cultivate.   75 *suggested* tempted.   76 *second fall* since the deposition of a King is as great a calamity as the fall of man [K].   79 *Divine* predict.
80 *Cam'st* Q²⁻⁵, F¹; Q¹: "canst."   82 *to breathe* in telling.   84 *weigh'd* balanced
against each other.   86 *vanities* follies.   90 *Post* travel quickly.   93 *Doth* . . .
me does not your message primarily concern me.

And am I last that knows it? O, thou thinkest
To serve me last, that I may longest keep   95
Thy sorrow in my breast. Come, ladies, go
To meet at London London's king in woe.
What, was I born to this, that my sad look
Should grace the triumph of great Bolingbroke?
Gard'ner, for telling me these news of woe,   100
Pray God the plants thou graft'st may never grow.

                              Exit [*with* Ladies].

GARD.   Poor Queen, so that thy state might be no worse,
I would my skill were subject to thy curse!
Here did she fall a tear; here in this place
I'll set a bank of rue, sour herb of grace.   105
Rue, even for ruth, here shortly shall be seen,
In the remembrance of a weeping queen.   *Exeunt.*

---

96 *Thy sorrow* the sorrow you report.   99 *grace* adorn.   *triumph* triumphal pro-
cession.   102 *so that . . . worse* if by that your condition could be improved.
104 *fall* let fall.   105 *herb of grace* Rue was called "herb of grace" because to
"rue" means to "repent' and repentance comes by grace of God [K].   106 *for ruth*
as a symbol of pity.

Act Four

◇◇◇

SCENE I. [*Westminster Hall.*]

Enter, as to the Parliament, Bolingbroke, Aumerle,
Northumberland, Percy, Fitzwater, Surrey, [*and an-*
other Lord, the Bishop of] Carlisle, Abbot of Westminster, Herald; Officers *and* Bagot.

BOLING.   Call forth Bagot.

                              [*Officers bring him forward.*]

Now, Bagot, freely speak thy mind,
What thou dost know of noble Gloucester's death;
Who wrought it with the King, and who perform'd
The bloody office of his timeless end.   5

BAGOT.   Then set before my face the Lord Aumerle.

BOLING.   Cousin, stand forth, and look upon that man.

BAGOT.   My Lord Aumerle, I know your daring tongue
Scorns to unsay what once it hath deliver'd.
In that dead time when Gloucester's death was plotted,   10
I heard you say, "Is not my arm of length,
That reacheth from the restful English court
As far as Calais to mine uncle's head?"
Amongst much other talk that very time
I heard you say that you had rather refuse   15
The offer of an hundred thousand crowns

IV.I.   4 *wrought it with the king* brought it about by influencing the King.   5
timeless untimely.   9 *deliver'd* reported.   10 *dead* dark and dismal (not deadly).
11 *of length* long.   12 *restful* calm, untroubled by Gloucester's intrigues.

73

Than Bolingbroke's return to England;
Adding withal, how blest this land would be
In this your cousin's death.

AUM.   Princes and noble lords,
What answer shall I make to this base man?   20
Shall I so much dishonour my fair stars
On equal terms to give him chastisement?
Either I must, or have mine honour soil'd
With the attainder of his slanderous lips.
There is my gage, the manual seal of death   25
That marks thee out for hell. I say thou liest,
And will maintain what thou hast said is false
In thy heart-blood, though being all too base
To stain the temper of my knightly sword.

BOLING. Bagot, forbear; thou shalt not take it up.   30

AUM. Excepting one, I would he were the best
In all this presence that hath mov'd me so.

FITZ. If that thy valour stand on sympathy,
There is my gage, Aumerle, in gage to thine.
By that fair sun which shows me where thou stand'st,   35
I heard thee say, and vauntingly thou spak'st it,
That thou wert cause of noble Gloucester's death.
If thou deniest it twenty times, thou liest,
And I will turn thy falsehood to thy heart,
Where it was forged, with my rapier's point.   40

AUM. Thou dar'st not, coward, live to see that day.

FITZ. Now, by my soul, I would it were this hour.

---

17 *Bolingbroke's return* for Bolingbroke to return.   18 *withal* besides.   20 *base* in rank.   21 *fair stars* high rank — as determined by the stars that ruled at my birth [K].   22 *him* Q³⁻⁵; Q¹: "them"; Q²: "my."   22 *On equal terms* in wager of battle.   *to* as to.   24 *attainder* stigma — with an allusion to the degradation and forfeiture that legally followed conviction of treason or felony [K].   25 *my gage* He throws down his glove.   25-6 *manual seal . . . hell* the warrant (sealed by the hand of Death) that damns thee to death and damnation [K]. The quibble on "manual" indicates that Aumerle's gage is a glove, rather than a hood, as Holinshed reports.   28-9 *though being . . . sword* Aumerle repeats his contempt for Bagot's rank and lineage. Bagot's blood, he asserts, will disgrace the sword of one of knightly rank [K].   *temper* (a) tempered steel (b) honourable quality.   30 *it*

AUM.   Fitzwater, thou art damn'd to hell for this.

PERCY.   Aumerle, thou liest. His honour is as true
         In this appeal as thou art all unjust;   45
         And that thou art so, there I throw my gage
         To prove it on thee to the extremest point
         Of mortal breathing. Seize it if thou dar'st.

AUM.   And if I do not, may my hands rot off
         And never brandish more revengeful steel   50
         Over the glittering helmet of my foe!

ANOTHER LORD. I task the earth to the like, forsworn Aumerle;
         And spur thee on with full as many lies
         As may be holloa'd in thy treacherous ear
         From sun to sun. There is my honour's pawn.   55
         Engage it to the trial, if thou dar'st.

AUM.   Who sets me else? By heaven, I'll throw at all!
         I have a thousand spirits in one breast
         To answer twenty thousand such as you.

SURREY. My Lord Fitzwater, I do remember well   60
         The very time Aumerle and you did talk.

FITZ.   'Tis very true. You were in presence then,
         And you can witness with me this is true.

SURREY. As false, by heaven, as heaven itself is true!

FITZ.   Surrey, thou liest.

SURREY.   Dishonourable boy!   65
         That lie shall lie so heavy on my sword
         That it shall render vengeance and revenge

---

the gage.   31 *one* Bolingbroke.   *best* highest in rank.   33 *If . . . sympathy* if
your valour insist on equality of rank in your opponent.   39 *turn* return.   40
rapier's The rapier was a gentleman's weapon in Shakespeare's time, though not
in that of King Richard [K].   45 *appeal* accusation.   *all unjust* completely false.
47–8 *extremest . . . breathing* death.   52 *task . . . like* I lay on the earth
the burden of bearing the like gage (Q¹; CAPELL, K: "I task thee to the like").   54
As CAPELL; QQ: "As it."   55 *sun to sun* CAPELL; Q¹: "sinne to sinne."   *pawn*
pledge   56 *Engage . . . trial* accept it by your pledge to meet me in combat [K].
57 *sets me* puts up stakes against me. The figure is from dicing.   *throw at all*
throw down gages (like wagers at dice) against all of you.   62 *in presence* in the
King's presence chamber at court.

Till thou the lie-giver and that lie do lie
In earth as quiet as thy father's skull.
In proof whereof there is my honour's pawn.   70
Engage it to the trial if thou dar'st.

FITZ.   How fondly dost thou spur a forward horse!
If I dare eat, or drink, or breathe, or live,
I dare meet Surrey in a wilderness,
And spit upon him whilst I say he lies,   75
And lies, and lies. There is my bond of faith
To tie thee to my strong correction.
As I intend to thrive in this new world,
Aumerle is guilty of my true appeal.
Besides, I heard the banish'd Norfolk say   80
That thou, Aumerle, didst send two of thy men
To execute the noble Duke at Calais.

AUM.   Some honest Christian trust me with a gage
That Norfolk lies. Here do I throw down this,
If he may be repeal'd to try his honour.   85

BOLING. These differences shall all rest under gage
Till Norfolk be repeal'd. Repeal'd he shall be
And, though mine enemy, restor'd again
To all his lands and signories. When he's return'd,
Against Aumerle we will enforce his trial.   90

CAR.   That honourable day shall ne'er be seen.
Many a time hath banish'd Norfolk fought
For Jesu Christ in glorious Christian field,
Streaming the ensign of the Christian cross
Against black pagans, Turks, and Saracens;   95
And, toil'd with works of war, retir'd himself
To Italy; and there, at Venice, gave
His body to that pleasant country's earth
And his pure soul unto his captain, Christ,

---

72 *fondly* foolishly. *forward* willing.   76 *my* Q³; not in Q¹.   *bond of faith* gage
(which he throws down).   78 *in this new world* under King Henry.   79 *appeal*
accusation.   84 *this* Some one has handed Aumerle a glove [ᴋ].   85 *repeal'd*
called back.   86 *under gage* as challenges.   89 *signories* estates.   90 *trial* in battle.   94 *Streaming* flying.   96 *toil'd* exhausted.   103–4 *bosom . . . Abraham* to
heavenly rest.   104 *appellants* accusers.   108. *plume-pluck'd* humbled, denuded

Under whose colours he had fought so long.   100

BOLING. Why, Bishop, is Norfolk dead?

CAR. As surely as I live, my lord.

BOLING. Sweet peace conduct his sweet soul to the bosom
Of good old Abraham! Lords appellants,
Your differences shall all rest under gage   105
Till we assign you to your days of trial.

Enter York [*attended*].

YORK. Great Duke of Lancaster, I come to thee
From plume-pluck'd Richard, who with willing soul
Adopts thee heir and his high sceptre yields
To the possession of thy royal hand.   110
Ascend his throne, descending now from him,
And long live Henry, fourth of that name!

BOLING. In God's name I'll ascend the regal throne.

CAR. Marry, God forbid!
Worst in this royal presence may I speak,   115
Yet best beseeming me to speak the truth.
Would God that any in this noble presence
Were enough noble to be upright judge
Of noble Richard! then true noblesse would
Learn him forbearance from so foul a wrong.   120
What subject can give sentence on his king?
And who sits here that is not Richard's subject?
Thieves are not judg'd but they are by to hear,
Although apparent guilt be seen in them;
And shall the figure of God's majesty,   125
His captain, steward, deputy elect,
Anointed, crowned, planted many years,
Be judg'd by subject and inferior breath,
And he himself not present? O, forfend it God

of his glory (referring possibly to Aesop's fable of the crow left in shame when
other birds had plucked away her stolen feathers).   111 *descending now from
him* which now falls to you as heir.   115 *Worst* of lowest rank.   116 *best . . .
truth* as a clergyman.   119 *noblesse* nobility.   120 *Learn* teach. *forbearance* to
refrain.   123 *judg'd* condemned.   124 *apparent* manifest.   125 *figure* image.
129 *forfend* forbid.

That, in a Christian climate, souls refin'd   130
Should show so heinous, black, obscene a deed!
I speak to subjects, and a subject speaks,
Stirr'd up by God, thus boldly for his king.
My Lord of Hereford here, whom you call king,
Is a foul traitor to proud Hereford's king;   135
And if you crown him, let me prophesy,
The blood of English shall manure the ground
And future ages groan for this foul act;
Peace shall go sleep with Turks and infidels,
And in this seat of peace tumultuous wars   140
Shall kin with kin and kind with kind confound;
Disorder, horror, fear, and mutiny
Shall here inhabit, and this land be call'd
The field of Golgotha and dead men's skulls.
O, if you raise this house against this house,   145
It will the woefullest division prove
That ever fell upon this cursed earth.
Prevent it, resist it, let it not be so,
Lest child, child's children cry against you woe.

NORTH. Well have you argued, sir; and for your pains   150
Of capital treason we arrest you here.
My Lord of Westminster, be it your charge
To keep him safely till his day of trial.
May it please you, lords, to grant the commons' suit.

BOLING. Fetch hither Richard, that in common view   155
He may surrender. So we shall proceed
Without suspicion.

YORK.   I will be his conduct.   *Exit.*

BOLING. Lords, you that here are under our arrest,
Procure your sureties for your days of answer.
Little are we beholding to your love,   160

---

130 *climate* region. *refin'd* purified (by Christianity).   131 *obscene* repulsive.
141 *Shall kin . . . confound* shall destroy kinsmen and fellow countrymen by the
hands of each other [K].   144 *Golgotha* Calvary. The deposition of a king is
linked poetically to the crucifixion. 146 *woefullest division* Carlisle is predicting
the Wars of the Roses.   148 *Prevent* forestall.   151 *Of* on a charge of.   154 *suit*
request that the causes of Richard's deposition be published.   156 *surrender*

And little look'd for at your helping hands.

Enter Richard *and* York, [*with* Officers
bearing the crown, &c.].

RICH.   Alack, why am I sent for to a king
Before I have shook off the regal thoughts
Wherewith I reign'd? I hardly yet have learn'd
To insinuate, flatter, bow, and bend my limbs.   165
Give sorrow leave awhile to tutor me
To this submission. Yet I well remember
The favours of these men. Were they not mine?
Did they not sometime cry "All hail!" to me?
So Judas did to Christ; but he, in twelve,   170
Found truth in all but one; I, in twelve thousand none.
God save the King! Will no man say amen?
Am I both priest and clerk? Well then, amen!
God save the King! although I be not he;
And yet amen, if heaven do think him me.   175
To do what service am I sent for hither?

YORK.   To do that office of thine own good will
Which tired majesty did make thee offer —
The resignation of thy state and crown
To Henry Bolingbroke.   180

RICH.   Give me the crown. Here, cousin, seize the crown.
Here, cousin,
On this side my hand, and on that side yours.
Now is this golden crown like a deep well
That owes two buckets, filling one another,   185
The emptier ever dancing in the air,
The other down, unseen, and full of water.
That bucket down and full of tears am I,
Drinking my griefs whilst you mount up on high.

abdicate.   157 *conduct* escort.   159 *sureties* men who will be responsbile for
your appearance.   160 *beholding* indebted.   168 *favours* (a) faces (b) acts of
friendship.   169 *sometime* once.   173 *clerk* whose duty it was to say "Amen"
after the priest's prayer.   178 *tired majesty* weariness with being king.   179 *state*
royal rank.   183 *and* Q⁴; not in F¹.   185 *owes* possesses.   *two buckets* The figure
of fortune's buckets occurs often in medieval literature.

BOLING.   I thought you had been willing to resign.   190

RICH.   My crown I am, but still my griefs are mine.
           You may my glories and my state depose,
           But not my griefs. Still am I king of those.

BOLING.   Part of your cares you give me with your crown.

RICH.   Your cares set up do not pluck my cares down.   195
           My care is loss of care, by old care done;
           Your care is gain of care, by new care won.
           The cares I give I have, though given away;
           They tend the crown, yet still with me they stay.

BOLING.   Are you contented to resign the crown?   200

RICH.   Ay, no; no, ay; for I must nothing be;
           Therefore no no, for I resign to thee.
           Now mark me how I will undo myself.
           I give this heavy weight from off my head
           And this unwieldy sceptre from my hand,   205
           The pride of kingly sway from out my heart.
           With mine own tears I wash away my balm,
           With mine own hands I give away my crown,
           With mine own tongue deny my sacred state,
           With mine own breath release all duteous oaths.   210
           All pomp and majesty I do forswear;
           My manors, rents, revenues I forgo;
           My acts, decrees, and statutes I deny.
           God pardon all oaths that are broke to me!
           God keep all vows unbroke are made to thee!   215
           Make me, that nothing have, with nothing griev'd,
           And thou with all pleas'd, that hast all achiev'd!

195–9 *Your cares . . . they stay* There is an elaborate pun on the two senses of
"care" — (a) trouble or sorrow (b) the worry or anxious care incident to high
office. But the sense is clear enough: "The fact that your cares (anxious responsibilities) are increased does not reduce my cares (sorrows). What troubles me is
that my old cares and anxieties as King have been lost; what gives you cause for
anxiety is the addition to your cares that comes from your new responsibilities"
[K].   198 *I have* because I sorrow for their loss.   199 *tend* go with.   201–2 *Ay,
no . . . no no* There is a troublesome pun on "ay" (printed "I" in the old texts)
and the pronoun "I." "My answer is both 'ay' and 'no'; for I am now forced to
be nothing — and consequently my 'ay' means 'no.' Therefore I answer 'no no'
— which means 'ay, ay' " [K].   203 *undo* (a) unmake (b) undress (another quib-

Long mayst thou live in Richard's seat to sit,
And soon lie Richard in an earthy pit!
God save King Harry, unking'd Richard says,　　220
And send him many years of sunshine days!
What more remains?

NORTH.　　　　　　　　　　No more, but that you read
These accusations and these grievous crimes
Committed by your person and your followers
Against the state and profit of this land,　　225
That, by confessing them, the souls of men
May deem that you are worthily depos'd.

RICH.　Must I do so? and must I ravel out
My weav'd-up follies? Gentle Northumberland,
If thy offences were upon record,　　230
Would it not shame thee in so fair a troop
To read a lecture of them? If thou wouldst,
There shouldst thou find one heinous article,
Containing the deposing of a king
And cracking the strong warrant of an oath,　　235
Mark'd with a blot, damn'd in the book of heaven.
Nay, all of you that stand and look upon
Whilst that my wretchedness doth bait myself,
Though some of you, with Pilate, wash your hands,
Showing an outward pity, yet you Pilates　　240
Have here deliver'd me to my sour cross,
And water cannot wash away your sin.

NORTH.　My lord, dispatch. Read o'er these articles.

RICH.　Mine eyes are full of tears; I cannot see.

---

ble).　207 *balm* consecrated oil.　210 *release all duteous oaths* discharge my
subjects from the obligation of honouring their oaths to me (F¹; Q⁴⁻⁵, K: "duty's
rites").　213 *deny* repeal (so far as they depend on me for their authority) [K].
215 *are made* that are made (F¹; Q⁴⁻⁵, K: "that swear").　220 *Harry* Q⁴⁻⁵; F¹;
"Henry."　225 *state and profit* well-regulated prosperity.　227 *worthily* deserv-
edly.　228 *ravel out* unravel.　229 *follies* F¹; Q⁴⁻⁵, K: "folly."　231 *troop* company.　232 *lecture* public reading, like a church sermon.　233 *article* item.
235 *oath* of fealty and allegiance to the lawful king.　236 *damn'd* condemned.
237 *upon* Q⁴⁻⁵; F¹: "upon me."　238 *bait* torment. The figure is from bear-baiting.
241 *sour* bitter.

And yet salt water blinds them not so much   245
But they can see a sort of traitors here.
Nay, if I turn mine eyes upon myself,
I find myself a traitor with the rest;
For I have given here my soul's consent
To undeck the pompous body of a king;   250
Made glory base, and sovereignty a slave,
Proud majesty a subject, state a peasant.

NORTH.   My lord —

RICH.   No lord of thine, thou haught insulting man,
Nor no man's lord. I have no name, no title —   255
No, not that name was given me at the font —
But 'tis usurp'd. Alack the heavy day,
That I have worn so many winters out
And know not now what name to call myself!
O that I were a mockery king of snow,   260
Standing before the sun of Bolingbroke
To melt myself away in water drops!
Good king, great king, and yet not greatly good,
An if my word be sterling yet in England,
Let it command a mirror hither straight,   265
That it may show me what a face I have
Since it is bankrout of his majesty.

BOLING. Go some of you and fetch a looking glass.

                                    [*Exit an* Attendant.]

NORTH.   Read o'er this paper while the glass doth come.

RICH.   Fiend, thou torments me ere I come to hell!   270

BOLING. Urge it no more, my Lord Northumberland.

NORTH.   The commons will not then be satisfied.

---

246 *sort* pack, gang (a term of contempt).   250 *pompous* stately, magnificent.
251 *and* Q⁴⁻⁵; F¹: "a."   254 *haught* haughty, arrogant.   255 *Nor no* Q⁴⁻⁵; F¹: "No
nor no."   256 *No, not . . . font* not even the name that was given me when I
was christened. Richard reasons with the logic of despair and completely "un-
does [unmakes] himself." The usurper has stripped him of his royalty, which
was his by right of birth, and so has destroyed his identity. If not King, how can
he be Richard? He is a nameless outcast [K].   There is no reason to suppose a
reference here to the legend circulated by Richard's enemies and recorded by

RICH.   They shall be satisfied. I'll read enough
         When I do see the very book indeed
         Where all my sins are writ, and that's myself.   275

                    Enter one with a glass.

         Give me the glass, and therein will I read.
         No deeper wrinkles yet? Hath sorrow struck
         So many blows upon this face of mine
         And made no deeper wounds? O flattering glass,
         Like to my followers in prosperity,   280
         Thou dost beguile me! Was this face the face
         That every day under his household roof
         Did keep ten thousand men? Was this the face
         That like the sun did make beholders wink?
         Was this the face that fac'd so many follies   285
         And was at last outfac'd by Bolingbroke?
         A brittle glory shineth in this face.
         As brittle as the glory is the face,

                    [Dashes the glass to the floor.]

         For there it is, crack'd in a hundred shivers.
         Mark, silent king, the moral of this sport —   290
         How soon my sorrow hath destroy'd my face.

BOLING. The shadow of your sorrow hath destroy'd
         The shadow of your face.

RICH.   Say that again.
         The shadow of my sorrow? Ha! let's see!
         'Tis very true: my grief lies all within;   295
         And these external manners of laments
         Are merely shadows to the unseen grief
         That swells with silence in the tortured soul.

Froissart that Richard was actually the bastard son of a priest of Bordeaux.
264 *be sterling* pass current.   **267** *bankrout* bankrupt. *his* its.   **276** *the* Q⁴⁻⁵; F¹:
"that."   **283** *keep* maintain.   **284** *wink* close their eyes.   **285** *Was* Q⁴⁻⁵; F¹: "Is."
285 *fac'd* countenanced.   **286** *And* Q⁴⁻⁵; F¹: "That." *outfac'd* discountenanced
and superseded.   **287** *brittle* fragile.   **289** *shivers* splinters.   **292-3** *The shadow
. . . face* the outward show (shadow) of your sorrow has destroyed the reflection
(shadow) of your face in the mirror, as one shadow may overshadow another.
296 *manners* forms (Q⁴⁻⁵; F¹: "manner"). *of laments* of lamentation.

        There lies the substance; and I thank thee, king,

        For thy great bounty that not only giv'st   300

        Me cause to wail, but teachest me the way

        How to lament the cause. I'll beg one boon,

        And then be gone and trouble you no more.

        Shall I obtain it?

BOLING.   Name it, fair cousin.

RICH.   Fair cousin? I am greater than a king;   305

        For when I was a king, my flatterers

        Were then but subjects; being now a subject,

        I have a king here to my flatterer.

        Being so great, I have no need to beg.

BOLING. Yet ask.   310

RICH.   And shall I have?

BOLING. You shall.

RICH.   Then give me leave to go.

BOLING. Whither?

RICH.   Whither you will, so I were from your sights.   315

BOLING. Go some of you, convey him to the Tower.

RICH.   O, good! Convey? Conveyors are you all,

        That rise thus nimbly by a true king's fall.

                   [Exit Richard *with some* Lords *and a*
                   Guard.]

BOLING. On Wednesday next we solemnly set down

        Our coronation. Lords, prepare yourselves.   320

                   Exeunt. Manent [the Abbott of] West-
                   minster, [the Bishop of] Carlisle, Au-
                   merle.

---

299 *There* in the soul.   300 *that* who, referring to Bolingbroke.   302 *boon* favour.
308 *to* for.   315 *so* provided that. *sights* the views of all the beholders.   316
convey escort.   317 *Conveyers* thieves, swindlers. To "convey" was a polite term
for "steal" [K].   319 *pageant* dramatic spectacle.   322-3*The woe . . . thorn* Again

ABBOT.   A woeful pageant have we here beheld.

CAR.   The woe's to come. The children yet unborn
         Shall feel this day as sharp to them as thorn.

AUM.   You holy clergymen, is there no plot
         To rid the realm of this pernicious blot?   325

ABBOT.   My lord,
         Before I freely speak my mind herein,
         You shall not only take the sacrament
         To bury mine intents, but also to effect
         Whatever I shall happen to devise.   330
         I see your brows are full of discontent,
         Your hearts of sorrow, and your eyes of tears.
         Come home with me to supper. I will lay
         A plot shall show us all a merry day.   *Exeunt.*

---

we have a prediction of the Wars of the Roses.   324 *no plot* no possible plan to
be devised. Not here used in an evil sense [K].   328 *take the sacrament* This was
done to increase the sacred obligation of an oath — especially an oath of secrecy
[K], 329 *bury* hide. *mine intents* what I intend.

Act Five

◇◇◇

SCENE I.

[London. A street leading to the Tower.]

Enter the Queen *with* Ladies, *her* Attendants.

QUEEN. This way the King will come. This is the way
To Julius Cæsar's ill-erected tower,
To whose flint bosom my condemned lord
Is doom'd a prisoner by proud Bolingbroke.
Here let us rest, if this rebellious earth   5
Have any resting for her true king's queen.

Enter Richard *and* Guard.

But soft, but see, or rather do not see,
My fair rose wither. Yet look up, behold,
That you in pity may dissolve to dew
And wash him fresh again with true-love tears.   10
Ah, thou the model where old Troy did stand,
Thou map of honour, thou King Richard's tomb,
And not King Richard! Thou most beauteous inn,
Why should hard-favour'd grief be lodg'd in thee
When triumph is become an alehouse guest?   15

V.I. 2 *Julius Cæsar's* A medieval tradition held that Julius Caesar had built the
Tower of London. *ill-erected* erected with evil results (not "poorly constructed").
3 *flint* merciless. 6 *resting* resting place. 11–12 *model . . . stand* as the ruins
of Troy show the outlines of that magnificent city, so you, in your misery, recall
to our minds what King Richard was in his days of splendour [K]. 12 *map of
honour* mere outline of former glory. 13–15 *Thou most . . . guest* Richard is
compared to a beautiful inn which entertains grief as a guest while Bolingbroke
is a common alehouse which entertains triumph. The figure is based upon the

RICH.   Join not with grief, fair woman, do not so,
        To make my end too sudden. Learn, good soul,
        To think our former state a happy dream;
        From which awak'd, the truth of what we are
        Shows us but this. I am sworn brother, sweet,   20
        To grim Necessity, and he and I
        Will keep a league till death. Hie thee to France
        And cloister thee in some religious house.
        Our holy lives must win a new world's crown,
        Which our profane hours here have thrown down.   25

QUEEN. What, is my Richard both in shape and mind
        Transform'd and weak'ned? Hath Bolingbroke depos'd
        Thine intellect? Hath he been in thy heart?
        The lion dying thrusteth forth his paw
        And wounds the earth, if nothing else, with rage   30
        To be o'erpow'r'd; and wilt thou pupil-like
        Take thy correction, mildly kiss the rod,
        And fawn on rage with base humility,
        Which art a lion and the king of beasts?

RICH.   A king of beasts indeed! If aught but beasts,   35
        I had been still a happy king of men.
        Good sometime queen, prepare thee hence for France.
        Think I am dead, and that even here thou takest,
        As from my deathbed, thy last living leave.
        In winter's tedious nights sit by the fire   40
        With good old folks, and let them tell thee tales
        Of woeful ages long ago betid;
        And ere thou bid good-night, to quite their griefs
        Tell thou the lamentable tale of me,
        And send the hearers weeping to their beds.   45

---

double meaning of "entertain": (a) receive a guest (b) harbour feeling. It is a common metaphor.   14 *hard-favour'd* ugly in features.   18 *state* condition of splendour.   20 *but this* only this miserable condition.   23 *religious house* convent.   24 *a new world's* heaven's.   25 *profane hours . . . down* our godless lives have caused us to lose in this world.   *thrown* two syllables, "throwen" (Q¹; F¹, K: "stricken").   31 *To be* at being.   32 *thy* F¹; Q¹: "the."   33 *rage* thy savage enemies.   37 *sometime* formerly (F¹; Q¹: "sometimes").   42 *Of . . . betid* which happened in ages long past.   43 *quite* requite, pay them for.   *griefs* tales of woe.

For why, the senseless brands will sympathize
The heavy accent of thy moving tongue
And in compassion weep the fire out;
And some will mourn in ashes, some coal-black,
For the deposing of a rightful king.   50

Enter Northumberland [*attended*].

NORTH. My lord, the mind of Bolingbroke is chang'd.
You must to Pomfret, not unto the Tower.
And, madam, there is order ta'en for you:
With all swift speed you must away to France.

RICH.   Northumberland, thou ladder wherewithal   55
The mounting Bolingbroke ascends my throne,
The time shall not be many hours of age
More than it is, ere foul sin gathering head
Shall break into corruption. Thou shalt think,
Though he divide the realm and give thee half,   60
It is too little, helping him to all.
And he shall think that thou, which know'st the way
To plant unrightful kings, wilt know again,
Being ne'er so little urg'd, another way,
To pluck him headlong from the usurped throne.   65
The love of wicked men converts to fear;
That fear to hate, and hate turns one or both
To worthy danger and deserved death.

NORTH. My guilt be on my head, and there an end!
Take leave and part, for you must part forthwith.   70

RICH.   Doubly divorc'd! Bad men, you violate
A twofold marriage — 'twixt my crown and me,

46–7 *For why . . . tongue* and with good reason, for even the insensate fire-
brands will be moved in accord with the mournful sound [K].   49 *mourn in
ashes* To scatter dust or ashes upon ones' head or to grovel in the dust or ashes
was an old ceremony of mourning [K].   52 *Pomfret* Pontefract Castle in Yorkshire.
53 *order ta'en* arrangements made.   55 *wherewithal* by means of which.   58
gathering head like a boil or carbuncle.   62 *And* ROWE; not in QQ, F¹.   61 *helping* having helped.   64 *urg'd* incited, tempted.   66 *converts* changes.   67 *one
or both* of the wicked men who have been in friendly relations [K].   68 *worthy*
well-merited.   74 *unkiss the oath* the marriage vow. A kiss was part of the
marriage ceremony. This kiss at parting is a sign that their union is at an end.
77 *pines the clime* lays waste the region.   78 *pomp* splendour.   80 *Hallowmas*
All Hallows, or All Saints' Day, the first of November (a dreary time of year, as

And then betwixt me and my married wife.
Let me unkiss the oath 'twixt thee and me;
And yet not so, for with a kiss 'twas made.   75
Part us, Northumberland — I towards the North,
Where shivering cold and sickness pines the clime;
My wife to France, from whence, set forth in pomp,
She came adorned hither like sweet May,
Sent back like Hallowmas or short'st of day.   80

QUEEN.   And must we be divided? Must we part?

RICH.   Ay, hand from hand, my love, and heart from heart.

QUEEN.   Banish us both, and send the King with me.

NORTH.   That were some love, but little policy.

QUEEN.   Then whither he goes, thither let me go.   85

RICH.   So two, together weeping, make one woe.
Weep thou for me in France, I for thee here.
Better far off than near be ne'er the near.
Go, count thy way with sighs; I mine with groans.

QUEEN.   So longest way shall have the longest moans.   90

RICH.   Twice for one step I'll groan, the way being short,
And piece the way out with a heavy heart.
Come, come, in wooing sorrow let's be brief,
Since, wedding it, there is such length in grief.
One kiss shall stop our mouths, and dumbly part.   95
Thus give I mine, and thus take I thy heart.

QUEEN.   Give me mine own again. 'Twere no good part
To take on me to keep and kill thy heart.

---

opposed to "sweet May"). *short'st of day* the winter solstice.   84 *North.* F¹; QQ
give the line to Richard. *little policy* poor statecraft.   88 *near be ne'er the near*
be near, and yet never the nearer for all that. Richard implies that they were to
be separated in any case [K].   94 *wedding it* when we come to take it for good
and all, as we must do; for when we part, you will have no husband, and I no
wife, except sorrow [K].   95 *dumbly part* make us part without bidding adieu.
96 *Thus . . . heart* That lovers exchange hearts in kissing is a common conceit
in Elizabethan love poetry.   97–8 *'Twere no . . . heart* it would be no good act
on my part to keep your heart with me, and, instead of guarding it, to kill it, as
my grief would be sure to do. "Keep" combines the senses of "keep with me" and
"guard" [K].

So, now I have mine own again, be gone,
That I may strive to kill it with a groan.   100

RICH.   We make woe wanton with this fond delay.
Once more adieu! The rest let sorrow say.   *Exeunt.*

◇◇◇◇◇◇◇◇◇◇◇◇◇◇◇

SCENE II.
[*London. The* Duke of York's *Palace.*]

Enter Duke of York *and the* Duchess.

DUCH.   My lord, you told me you would tell the rest,
When weeping made you break the story off
Of our two cousins' coming into London.

YORK.   Where did I leave?

DUCH.   At that sad stop, my lord,
Where rude misgoverned hands from windows' tops   5
Threw dust and rubbish on King Richard's head.

YORK.   Then, as I said, the Duke, great Bolingbroke,
Mounted upon a hot and fiery steed
Which his aspiring rider seem'd to know,
With slow but stately pace kept on his course,   10
Whilst all tongues cried "God save thee, Bolingbroke!"
You would have thought the very windows spake,
So many greedy looks of young and old
Through casements darted their desiring eyes
Upon his visage; and that all the walls   15
With painted imagery had said at once

---

101 *We . . . delay* in this childish delay we are merely indulging our woe by playing with it in fanciful talk which is of no avail [K].

V.II. 3 *cousins* Richard and Bolingbroke.   5 *misgoverned* unruly.   *windows' tops* upper windows.   16 *painted imagery* Human figures labelled with words or phrases which they were supposed to be speaking, were common in the hangings (tapestry or painted cloth) that lined chamber walls. On festive occasions such hangings were often displayed on houses. York was reminded of them by the sight of the house walls with their windows crowded with shouting inhabitants [K].   19 *lower* bending lower.   21 *still* constantly.   24 *well-grac'd* (a) graceful

"Jesu preserve thee! Welcome, Bolingbroke!"
Whilst he, from the one side to the other turning,
Bareheaded, lower than his proud steed's neck,
Bespake them thus, "I thank you, countrymen."   20
And thus still doing, thus he pass'd along.

DUCH.   Alack, poor Richard! Where rode he the whilst?

YORK.   As in a theatre the eyes of men,
After a well-grac'd actor leaves the stage,
Are idly bent on him that enters next,   25
Thinking his prattle to be tedious,
Even so, or with much more contempt, men's eyes
Did scowl on gentle Richard. No man cried "God save him!"
No joyful tongue gave him his welcome home,
But dust was thrown upon his sacred head;   30
Which with such gentle sorrow he shook off,
His face still combating with tears and smiles
(The badges of his grief and patience),
That, had not God for some strong purpose steel'd
The hearts of men, they must perforce have melted   35
And barbarism itself have pitied him.
But heaven hath a hand in these events,
To whose high will we bound our calm contents.
To Bolingbroke are we sworn subjects now,
Whose state and honour I for aye allow.   40

Enter Aumerle.

DUCH.   Here comes my son Aumerle.

YORK.   Aumerle that was;
But that is lost for being Richard's friend,
And, madam, you must call him Rutland now.

(b) well received.   25 *idly* with indifference.   31 *gentle* noble and magnanimous.
33 *badges* outward signs.   36 *barbarism itself* even barbarians.   38 *To whose
. . . contents* and we must rest happy and contented within whatever limits
heaven's will may confine the satisfaction of our wishes; we must accept with
calm submission the limits that God's will sets for our happiness [K].   40 *state*
high rank.   *allow* accept and approve.   41 *Aumerle that was* Holinshed records
that Aumerle, along with Surrey and Exeter, was deprived of his title by Henry's
first parliament because of his support of Richard, although he was allowed to
retain the title of Earl of Rutland.

I am in parliament pledge for his truth
And lasting fealty to the new-made king.   45

DUCH.   Welcome, my son. Who are the violets now
          That strew the green lap of the new-come spring?

AUM.   Madam, I know not, nor I greatly care not.
          God knows I had as lief be none as one.

YORK.   Well, bear you well in this new spring of time,   50
          Lest you be cropp'd before you come to prime.
          What news from Oxford? Do these justs and triumphs hold?

AUM.   For aught I know, my lord, they do.

YORK.   You will be there, I know.

AUM.   If God prevent not, I purpose so.   55

YORK.   What seal is that that hangs without thy bosom?
          Yea, look'st thou pale? Let me see the writing.

AUM.   My lord, 'tis nothing.

YORK.   No matter then who see it.
          I will be satisfied; let me see the writing.

AUM.   I do beseech your Grace to pardon me.   60
          It is a matter of small consequence
          Which for some reasons I would not have seen.

YORK.   Which for some reasons, sir, I mean to see.
          I fear, I fear —

DUCH.   What should you fear?
          'Tis nothing but some bond that he is ent'red into   65
          For gay apparel 'gainst the triumph day.

YORK.   Bound to himself? What doth he with a bond
          That he is bound to? Wife, thou art a fool.
          Boy, let me see the writing.

---

46 *violets* newly created nobles.   47 *Strew . . . spring* are the new favourites at
court. Bolingbroke is implicitly compared to the sun under whose beams the new
favourites will bloom.   49 *none* not one of them.   50 *bear you* conduct yourself.
51 *cropp'd* like a plant. *prime* full bloom.   52 *Do these . . . hold* are the plans
for tournaments (justs) and triumphal processions (triumphs) settled.   56 *seal*
The seal of a document was affixed to a label — a strip of parchment that hung
beneath its lower border [K].   65 *bond* for payment of a debt.   *is ent'red*

AUM.   I do beseech you pardon me. I may not show it.   70

YORK.   I will be satisfied. Let me see it, I say.

> *He plucks it out of his bosom and reads it.*

Treason, foul treason! Villain! traitor! slave!

DUCH.   What is the matter, my lord?

YORK.   Ho! who is within there?

> [*Enter a* Servant.]

Saddle my horse.
God for his mercy, what treachery is here!   75

DUCH.   Why, what is it, my lord?

YORK.   Give me my boots, I say. Saddle my horse.

> [*Exit* Servant.]

Now, by mine honour, by my life, by my troth,
I will appeach the villain.

DUCH.   What is the matter?

YORK.   Peace, foolish woman.   80

DUCH.   I will not peace. What is the matter, Aumerle?

AUM.   Good mother, be content. It is no more
Than my poor life must answer.

DUCH.   Thy life answer?

YORK.   Bring me my boots! I will unto the King.

> *His* Man *enters with his boots.*

DUCH.   Strike him, Aumerle. Poor boy, thou art amaz'd. —   85
Hence, villain! Never more come in my sight.

YORK   Give me my boots, I say!   [Servant *does so and exit.*]

---

into has signed.   66 *'gainst* in preparation for.   67–8 *What doth . . . bound to*
Such a bond would of course be in the possession of the creditor, not the debtor
[K].   75 *God for* I pray God for.   78 *troth* faith to God and man.   79 *appeach*
inform against.   81 *peace* keep my peace.   82 *content* calm.   83 *answer* answer
for.   85 *amaz'd* dumfounded. She thinks Aumerle too stupefied to strike the
servant.   86 *villain* the servant.

DUCH. Why, York, what wilt thou do?
Wilt thou not hide the trespass of thine own?
Have we more sons? or are we like to have?   90
Is not my teeming date drunk up with time?
And wilt thou pluck my fair son from mine age
And rob me of a happy mother's name?
Is he not like thee? Is he not thine own?

YORK. Thou fond mad woman,   95
Wilt thou conceal this dark conspiracy?
A dozen of them here have ta'en the sacrament,
And interchangeably set down their hands,
To kill the King at Oxford.

DUCH.   He shall be none;
We'll keep him here. Then what is that to him?   100

YORK. Away, fond woman! Were he twenty times
My son, I would appeach him.

DUCH.   Hadst thou groan'd for him
As I have done, thou wouldst be more pitiful.
But now I know thy mind. Thou dost suspect
That I have been disloyal to thy bed   105
And that he is a bastard, not thy son.
Sweet York, sweet husband, be not of that mind!
He is as like thee as a man may be,
Not like to me, or any of my kin,
And yet I love him.

YORK.   Make way, unruly woman! *Exit.*   110

DUCH. After, Aumerle! Mount thee upon his horse,
Spur post and get before him to the King,
And beg thy pardon ere he do accuse thee.

91 *teeming date* period of childbearing. *drunk up* exhausted. 95 *fond* foolish.
98 *interchangeably . . . hands* signed reciprocally, so that each held an indenture
signed by all of the others. 99 *none* not one of them. 102 *appeach* inform
against. *groan'd* suffered the pains of childbirth. 111 *his horse* one of his
horses. There is no need to assume — with some editors — that Aumerle steals his
father's horse. 112 *post* posthaste.
V.III. 1 *unthrifty* dissolute, prodigal. 3 *plague* calamity. The evil ways of the
young prince were generally regarded as God's punishment for Bolingbroke's

I'll not be long behind. Though I be old,
I doubt not but to ride as fast as York;   115
And never will I rise up from the ground
Till Bolingbroke have pardon'd thee. Away, be gone!

Exeunt.

◇◇◇◇◇◇◇◇◇◇◇◇◇◇◇◇

SCENE III. [*Windsor Castle.*]

Enter King [Henry], Percy, *and other* Lords.

KING H. Can no man tell me of my unthrifty son?
'Tis full three months since I did see him last.
If any plague hang over us, 'tis he.
I would to God, my lords, he might be found.
Inquire at London, 'mongst the taverns there,   5
For there, they say, he daily doth frequent,
With unrestrained loose companions,
Even such, they say, as stand in narrow lanes
And beat our watch and rob our passengers,
Which he, young wanton and effeminate boy,   10
Takes on the point of honour to support
So dissolute a crew.

PERCY. My lord, some two days since I saw the Prince
And told him of those triumphs held at Oxford.

KING H. And what said the gallant?   15

PERCY. His answer was, he would unto the stews,
And from the common'st creature pluck a glove
And wear it as a favour, and with that
He would unhorse the lustiest challenger.

---

usurpation of the throne.   6 *frequent* resort.   7 *unrestrained loose* lawless and
wild.   *companions* fellows (in a contemptuous sense).   9 *watch* night watchmen.
passengers passers-by, travellers.   *which* whom, the companions.   10 *wanton*
spoiled child (a noun).   *effeminate* self-indulgent, unwilling to accept the responsibilities of manhood.   14 *held* to be held.   16 *stews* brothels.   18 *favour* token
of a lady's favour, commonly carried by knights in tournaments.   19 *lustiest* most
stalwart.

KING H.   As dissolute as desperate! Yet through both   20
          I see some sparks of better hope, which elder years
          May happily bring forth. But who comes here?

                    Enter Aumerle, *amazed.*

AUM.   Where is the King?

KING H.   What means our cousin, that he stares and looks
          So wildly?   25

AUM.   God save your Grace! I do beseech your Majesty
          To have some conference with your Grace alone.

KING H.   Withdraw yourselves and leave us here alone.

                              [*Exeunt* Percy *and* Lords.]

          What is the matter with our cousin now?

AUM.   For ever may my knees grow to the earth,   [*Kneels.*]
          My tongue cleave to the roof within my mouth,
          Unless a pardon ere I rise or speak.

KING H.   Intended, or committed, was this fault?
          If on the first, how heinous e'er it be,
          To win thy after-love I pardon thee.   35

AUM.   Then give me leave that I may turn the key,
          That no man enter till my tale be done.

KING H.   Have thy desire.

                    [Aumerle *locks the door.*] *The* Duke
                    of York *knocks at the door and crieth.*

YORK.   (*within*) My liege, beware! look to thyself!
          Thou hast a traitor in thy presence there.   40

KING H.   Villain, I'll make thee safe.   [*Draws.*]

---

22 *happily* perhaps. *amazed* distraught.   34 *on the first* intended, rather than
committed.   35 *after-love* gratitude and future loyalty.   41 *safe* harmless.   43
secure unsuspecting, overconfident.   44 *Shall . . . face* must I, because of my
love and loyalty, speak treason (call you a fool) to your face.   50 *haste . . . show*
breathlessness, from hurrying, prevents me from explaining.   51 *pass'd* already
given.   53 *hand* handwriting.   57 *Forget to pity him* ignore the pardon you
have given him.   58 *Serpent . . . heart* An allusion to the old fable of the man

AUM.	Stay thy revengeful hand; thou hast no cause to fear.	
YORK.	(*within*) Open the door, secure foolhardy king!	
	Shall I for love speak treason to thy face?	
	Open the door, or I will break it open!	45

Enter York.

KING H.	What is the matter, uncle? Speak.	
	Recover breath; tell us how near is danger,	
	That we may arm us to encounter it.	
YORK.	Peruse this writing here, and thou shalt know	
	The treason that my haste forbids me show.	50
AUM.	Remember, as thou read'st, thy promise pass'd.	
	I do repent me. Read not my name there.	
	My heart is not confederate with my hand.	
YORK.	It was, villain, ere thy hand did set it down.	
	I tore it from the traitor's bosom, King.	55
	Fear, and not love, begets his penitence.	
	Forget to pity him, lest thy pity prove	
	A serpent that will sting thee to the heart.	
KING H.	O heinous, strong, and bold conspiracy!	
	O loyal father of a treacherous son!	60
	Thou sheer, immaculate, and silver fountain,	
	From whence this stream through muddy passages	
	Hath held his current and defil'd himself!	
	Thy overflow of good converts to bad,	
	And thy abundant goodness shall excuse	65
	This deadly blot in thy digressing son.	
YORK.	So shall my virtue be his vice's bawd,	
	And he shall spend mine honour with his shame,	
	As thriftless sons their scraping father's gold.	

---

who warmed a half-frozen serpent by putting it in the bosom of his garment and was stung to death by the snake [K].   59 *strong* flagrant.   61 *sheer* pure.   62 *this stream* (indicating Aumerle).   64 *overflow* excess.   *converts* changes (in my son).   66 *blot* blemish.   *digressing* wayward.   68 *he shall . . . shame* since his shameful treason will always disgrace my honourable loyalty. York dwells upon this idea in the rest of his speech: only Aumerle's death can establish his father's good faith [K].   69 *scraping* hoarding.

Mine honour lives when his dishonour dies,   70
Or my sham'd life in his dishonour lies.
Thou kill'st me in his life; giving him breath,
The traitor lives, the true man's put to death.

DUCH.   *(within)* What ho, my liege! For God's sake let me in!

KING H.   What shrill-voic'd suppliant makes this eager cry?   75

DUCH.   *(within)* A woman, and thine aunt, great King. 'Tis I.
Speak with me, pity me, open the door!
A beggar begs that never begg'd before.

KING H.   Our scene is alt'red from a serious thing,
And now chang'd to "The Beggar and the King."   80
My dangerous cousin, let your mother in.
I know she is come to pray for your foul sin.

YORK.   If thou do pardon, whosoever pray,
More sins for this forgiveness prosper may.
This fest'red joint cut off, the rest rest sound;   85
This let alone will all the rest confound.

Enter Duchess.

DUCH.   O King, believe not this hard-hearted man!
Love loving not itself, none other can.

YORK.   Thou frantic woman, what dost thou make here?
Shall thy old dugs once more a traitor rear?   90

DUCH.   Sweet York, be patient. Hear me, gentle liege.
                                    [Kneels.]

KING H.   Rise up, good aunt.

DUCH.   Not yet, I thee beseech.
For ever will I walk upon my knees,
And never see day that the happy sees,
Till thou give joy, until thou bid me joy   95
By pardoning Rutland, my transgressing boy.

---

70 *lives* comes to life.   71 *lies* is involved in.   76 *thine* QQ; F¹, K: "thy."   79
Our scene the course of our drama.   80 *The Beggar and the King* a punning
allusion to the old song of "King Cophetua and the Beggar Maid" [K].   85 *rest
rest* others will remain.   86 *confound* destroy.   88 *Love . . . can* since he
has no love for Aumerle, his own flesh and blood, it is impossible that he should
love anybody — even his king [K].   89 *make* do.   91 *patient* calm.   93 *walk*

AUM.	Unto my mother's prayers I bend my knee. [*Kneels.*]	
YORK.	Against them both my true joints bended be. [*Kneels.*]	
	Ill mayst thou thrive if thou grant any grace!	
DUCH.	Pleads he in earnest? Look upon his face.	100
	His eyes do drop no tears, his prayers are in jest;	
	His words come from his mouth, ours from our breast.	
	He prays but faintly and would be denied;	
	We pray with heart and soul and all beside:	
	His weary joints would gladly rise, I know;	105
	Our knees shall kneel till to the ground they grow.	
	His prayers are full of false hypocrisy;	
	Ours of true zeal and deep integrity.	
	Our prayers do outpray his; then let them have	
	That mercy which true prayer ought to have.	110
KING H.	Good aunt, stand up.	
DUCH.	Nay, do not say "stand up."	
	Say "pardon" first, and afterwards "stand up."	
	An if I were thy nurse, thy tongue to teach,	
	"Pardon" should be the first word of thy speech.	
	I never long'd to hear a word till now.	115
	Say "pardon," King; let pity teach thee how.	
	The word is short, but not so short as sweet;	
	No word like "pardon" for kings' mouths so meet.	
YORK.	Speak it in French, King. Say "Pardonne moi."	
DUCH.	Dost thou teach pardon pardon to destroy?	120
	Ah, my sour husband, my hard-hearted lord,	
	That sets the word itself against the word!	
	Speak "pardon" as 'tis current in our land;	
	The chopping French we do not understand.	
	Thine eye begins to speak, set thy tongue there;	125
	Or in thy piteous heart plant thou thine ear,	

---

upon my knees a traditional form of penance.   97 *Unto* in support of.   98 *true* loyal.   106 *shall* F¹; QQ: "still."   111 *King H* F¹; Q¹ gives the line to York.   118 *meet* proper   119 *Pardonne moi* a courteous form of refusal.   121 *sour* bitter. 122 *sets . . . word* makes the word "pardon" contradict itself.   124 *chopping* changeable, ambiguous.   125 *speak* express pity.   126 *in thy . . . ear* listen to what your pitying heart is saying.

	That hearing how our plaints and prayers do pierce,	
	Pity may move thee "pardon" to rehearse.	
KING H.	Good aunt, stand up.	
DUCH.	I do not sue to stand.	
	Pardon is all the suit I have in hand.	130
KING H.	I pardon him as God shall pardon me.	
DUCH.	O happy vantage of a kneeling knee!	
	Yet am I sick for fear. Speak it again.	
	Twice saying 'pardon' doth not pardon twain,	
	But makes one pardon strong.	
KING H.	With all my heart	135
	I pardon him.	
DUCH.	A god on earth thou art. [*Rises.*]	
KING H.	But for our trusty brother-in-law and the Abbot,	
	With all the rest of that consorted crew,	
	Destruction straight shall dog them at the heels.	
	Good uncle, help to order several powers,	140
	To Oxford, or where'er these traitors are.	
	They shall not live within this world, I swear,	
	But I will have them, if I once know where.	
	Uncle, farewell; and, cousin, adieu.	
	Your mother well hath pray'd, and prove you true.	145
DUCH.	Come, my old son. I pray God make thee new.	

Exeunt.

◇◇◇◇◇◇◇◇◇◇◇◇◇◇◇◇

SCENE IV. [*Windsor Castle.*]

Enter Sir Pierce Exton *and* Servant.

EXTON.   Didst thou not mark the King, what words he spake?

---

127 *pierce* pronounced to rhyme with "rehearse."   128 *rehearse* repeat.   132
vantage advantage.   137 *for* as for.   *brother in law* the Duke of Exeter, married
to Henry's sister, Elizabeth.   *Abbot* of Westminster.   145 *prove you* may you
prove.   146 *old* referring not to his age, but to his character which she hopes
will be made new. There is an echo here of the baptismal service.

V.IV. 5 *urg'd it twice together* repeated it for emphasis.   7 *wishtly* intently,
longingly.   8 *who* one who.   11 *rid* get rid of.

"Have I no friend will rid me of this living fear?"
Was it not so?

MAN.   These were his very words.

EXTON.   "Have I no friend?" quoth he. He spake it twice
And urg'd it twice together, did he not?   5

MAN.   He did.

EXTON.   And speaking it, he wishtly look'd on me,
As who should say, "I would thou wert the man
That would divorce this terror from my heart!"
Meaning the king at Pomfret. Come, let's go.   10
I am the King's friend, and will rid his foe.   *Exeunt.*

◇◇◇◇◇◇◇◇◇◇◇◇◇◇◇◇◇

SCENE V. [*Pomfret Castle.*]

Enter Richard, *alone.*

RICH.   I have been studying how I may compare
This prison where I live unto the world;
And, for because the world is populous,
And here is not a creature but myself,
I cannot do it. Yet I'll hammer it out.   5
My brain I'll prove the female to my soul,
My soul the father; and these two beget
A generation of still-breeding thoughts;
And these same thoughts people this little world,
In humours like the people of this world,   10
For no thought is contented. The better sort,

V.v. 3 *for because* for the reason that.   5 *hammer it out* puzzle it out (a common Elizabethan expression).   6–10 *My brain . . . world* my feelings (the emo-
tions of my soul) act upon my brain, and the result is — thoughts. These thoughts
are still-breeding (they incessantly produce other thoughts); and thus this
little world (my prison) is populated by thoughts which resemble, in their dis-
positions, the people of the actual world; for they are never quite happy and
contented [K].

As thoughts of things divine, are intermix'd
With scruples, and do set the word itself
Against the word:
As thus, "Come, little ones," and then again,   15
"It is as hard to come as for a camel
To thread the postern of a small needle's eye."
Thoughts tending to ambition, they do plot
Unlikely wonders — how these vain weak nails
May tear a passage through the flinty ribs   20
Of this hard world, my ragged prison walls;
And, for they cannot, die in their own pride.
Thoughts tending to content flatter themselves
That they are not the first of fortune's slaves,
Nor shall not be the last; like seely beggars   25
Who, sitting in the stocks, refuge their shame,
That many have, and others must sit there.
And in this thought they find a kind of ease,
Bearing their own misfortunes on the back
Of such as have before endur'd the like.   30
Thus play I in one person many people,
And none contented. Sometimes am I king:
Then treasons make me wish myself a beggar,
And so I am. Then crushing penury
Persuades me I was better when a king;   35
Then am I king'd again; and by-and-by
Think that I am unking'd by Bolingbroke,
And straight am nothing. But whate'er I be,
Nor I, nor any man that but man is,
With nothing shall be pleas'd till he be eas'd   40

---

13 *scruples* doubts and difficulties.   13–14 *set . . . word* set one passage of the
Bible against another which contradicts it.   15 *Come, little ones* MATTHEW, xix,
14.   16–17 *It is . . . eye* MATTHEW, xix, 24.   *postern* a small back gate.   20 *ribs*
walls.   21 *ragged* rough.   22 *for* because.   *pride* prime.   25 *seely* silly, simple-
minded.   26 *refuge their shame* escape their sense of shame by thinking.   36
king'd made a king.   37 *unking'd* deposed.   40 *With . . . pleas'd* shall never be
fully satisfied with anything in this life [K].   41 *being nothing* death.   46 *check*
find fault with.   *disordered* out of tune.   *string* stringed instrument.   47 *concord*
harmony, music.   *state and time* government of the realm and of my life.   50
numb'ring clock clock showing hours and minutes (as opposed to an hourglass).
51–4 *My thoughts . . . tears* every minute of my life has its own sad thought that
makes me sigh. By these sighs (which are the ticks of the clock) my thoughts com-

With being nothing.   *The music plays.*
               Music do I hear?
Ha, ha! keep time. How sour sweet music is
When time is broke and no proportion kept!
So is it in the music of men's lives.
And here have I the daintiness of ear   45
To check time broke in a disordered string;
But, for the concord of my state and time,
Had not an ear to hear my true time broke.
I wasted time, and now doth time waste me;
For now hath time made me his numb'ring clock: 50
My thoughts are minutes; and with sighs they jar
Their watches on unto mine eyes, the outward watch,
Whereto my finger, like a dial's point,
Is pointing still, in cleansing them from tears.
Now, sir, the sound that tells what hour it is   55
Are clamorous groans, that strike upon my heart,
Which is the bell. So sighs and tears and groans
Show minutes, times, and hours. But my time
Runs posting on in Bolingbroke's proud joy,
While I stand fooling here, his Jack o' th' clock.   60
This music mads me. Let it sound no more;
For though it have holp madmen to their wits,
In me it seems it will make wise men mad.
Yet blessing on his heart that gives it me!
For 'tis a sign of love, and love to Richard   65
Is a strange brooch in this all-hating world.

Enter a Groom *of the stable.*

---

municate their wakefulness to my eyes. My eyes are the "outward watch" (the marks round the clock's dial) and to these my finger (like the minute hand) always points, for with every sigh it wipes away a tear [K].   55 *sound that tells* Q¹; POPE, K: "sounds that tell."   58 *times* divisions of the hour. *time* life.   59 *Runs . . . joy* my life (of sorrow) runs on with speed in the joyful reign of Bolingbroke, and I, in the meantime, stand here playing with words, and serve only to record (with my groans) the hours of his reign [K].   60 *Jack o' th' clock* a grotesque human figure that stands outside the clockcase and strikes the hours on the bell [K].   62 *holp . . . wits* The beneficial effect of music in the treatment of insanity is an ancient theory [K]. *holp* helped.   63 *wise* sane.   66 *strange brooch* rare jewel. Brooches were worn in hats.   66 *all-hating* in which everyone hates me.

GROOM. Hail, royal prince!

RICH.   Thanks, noble peer.
        The cheapest of us is ten groats too dear.
        What art thou? and how comest thou hither,
        Where no man never comes but that sad dog   70
        That brings me food to make misfortune live?

GROOM. I was a poor groom of thy stable, King,
        When thou wert king; who, travelling towards York,
        With much ado, at length, have gotten leave
        To look upon my sometimes royal master's face.   75
        O, how it ern'd my heart when I beheld,
        In London streets, that coronation day,
        When Bolingbroke rode on roan Barbary,
        That horse that thou so often hast bestrid,
        That horse that I so carefully have dress'd!   80

RICH.   Rode he on Barbary? Tell me, gentle friend,
        How went he under him?

GROOM. So proudly as if he disdain'd the ground.

RICH.   So proud that Bolingbroke was on his back!
        That jade hath eat bread from my royal hand;   85
        This hand hath made him proud with clapping him.
        Would he not stumble? would he not fall down
        (Since pride must have a fall) and break the neck
        Of that proud man that did usurp his back?
        Forgiveness, horse! Why do I rail on thee,   90
        Since thou, created to be aw'd by man,
        Wast born to bear? I was not made a horse;
        And yet I bear a burden like an ass,
        Spurr'd, gall'd and tir'd by jauncing Bolingbroke.

                    Enter Keeper, *with a dish.*

---

67 *peer* equal.   68 *The cheapest . . . dear* A groat was fourpence. A royal was
a coin worth ten shillings (120 pence); a noble was worth six shillings and eight-
pence (80 pence). The difference between a royal and a noble, then, would be ten
groats (40 pence). The King plays with the word "peer." He means that "the
cheapest" of them (himself, the prisoner) has become the "peer" or equal of
a groom. Richard is emphasizing his own depreciation; to call him "royal" is to
price him "ten groats" too high [K].   70 *sad dog* dismal fellow.   75 *sometimes*

KEEPER. Fellow, give place. Here is no longer stay.   95

RICH.   If thou love me, 'tis time thou wert away.

GROOM. What my tongue dares not, that my heart shall say.

Exit.

KEEPER. My lord, will't please you to fall to?

RICH.   Taste of it first, as thou art wont to do.

KEEPER. My lord, I dare not. Sir Pierce of Exton,   100
        Who lately came from the King, commands the contrary.

RICH.   The devil take Henry of Lancaster, and thee!
        Patience is stale, and I am weary of it.

[Beats the Keeper.]

KEEPER. Help, help, help!

Exton and Servants, *the Murderers,
rush in.*

RICH.   How now! What means death in this rude assault?   105
        Villain, thy own hand yields thy death's instrument.

[Snatches a weapon from a Servant
and kills him.]

Go thou and fill another room in hell.

[Kills another.] Here Exton *strikes
him down.*

That hand shall burn in never-quenching fire
That staggers thus my person. Exton, thy fierce hand
Hath with the King's blood stain'd the King's own
        land.   .   110
Mount, mount, my soul! thy seat is up on high;
Whilst my gross flesh sinks downward, here to die.

[Dies.]

---

former.   76 *ern'd* grieved.   80 *dress'd* groomed.   83 *he* Q¹; F¹, K: "he had."
85 *jade* nag (contemptuous term for "horse").   *eat* eaten.   86 *clapping* patting.
94 *gall'd* made sore.   *jauncing* making the horse prance.   98 *fall to* begin eating.
99 *art wont* are accustomed.   105 *What . . . assault* Death is personified. "What
does Death mean by assailing me so violently? I had thought he would let me
'pine away' with grief" [K]. This is one possible explanation. The line is obscure
and has been variously interpreted.   107 *room* place.

EXTON. As full of valour as of royal blood.
Both have I spill'd. O, would the deed were good!
For now the devil, that told me I did well,   115
Says that this deed is chronicled in hell.
This dead king to the living king I'll bear.
Take hence the rest, and give them burial here.

Exeunt.

◇◇◇◇◇◇◇◇◇◇◇◇◇◇◇◇

SCENE VI. [*Windsor Castle.*]

Flourish. Enter Bolingbroke [*as* King], *the* Duke of
York, *with other* Lords, *and* Attendants.

KING. Kind uncle York, the latest news we hear
Is that the rebels have consum'd with fire
Our town of Ciceter in Gloucestershire;
But whether they be ta'en or slain we hear not.

Enter Northumberland.

Welcome, my lord. What is the news?   5

NORTH. First, to thy sacred state wish I all happiness.
The next news is, I have to London sent
The heads of Oxford, Salisbury, Blunt, and Kent.
The manner of their taking may appear
At large discoursed in this paper here.   10

KING. We thank thee, gentle Percy, for thy pains
And to thy worth will add right worthy gains.

Enter Lord Fitzwater.

FITZ. My lord, I have from Oxford sent to London
The heads of Brocas and Sir Bennet Seely,

V.VI. 2 *consum'd* destroyed.   3 *Ciceter* Cirencester. The Q¹ spelling indicates the
pronunciation in Shakespeare's day.   6 *state* royalty.   9 *taking* capture.   10 *at
large discoursed* explained in full.   12 *worth* (a) deserts (b) possessions.   *worthy*
(a) well-deserved (b) valuable.   15 *consorted* associated.   18 *wot* know.   20 *clog
of conscience* burden of a guilty conscience. The metaphor is from the wooden

Two of the dangerous consorted traitors   15
That sought at Oxford thy dire overthrow.

KING.   Thy pains, Fitzwater, shall not be forgot.
Right noble is thy merit, well I wot.

Enter Henry Percy *and* [*the* Bishop
of] Carlisle.

PERCY.   The grand conspirator, Abbot of Westminster,
With clog of conscience and sour melancholy   20
Hath yielded up his body to the grave;
But here is Carlisle living, to abide
Thy kingly doom and sentence of his pride.

KING.   Carlisle, this is your doom:
Choose out some secret place, some reverend room, 25
More than thou hast, and with it joy thy life.
So, as thou liv'st in peace, die free from strife;
For though mine enemy thou hast ever been,
High sparks of honour in thee have I seen.

Enter Exton, *with* [Attendants *bearing*] *a coffin.*

EXTON.   Great King, within this coffin I present   30
Thy buried fear. Herein all breathless lies
The mightiest of thy greatest enemies,
Richard of Bordeaux, by me hither brought.

KING.   Exton, I thank thee not; for thou hast wrought
A deed of slander, with thy fatal hand,   35
Upon my head and all this famous land.

EXTON.   From your own mouth, my lord, did I this deed.

KING.   They love not poison that do poison need,
Nor do I thee. Though I did wish him dead,
I hate the murderer, love him murdered.   40

---

weight (clog) used to keep animals from straying.   22 *abide* await.   23 *doom*
sentence.   25 *secret place* place of retirement — such as a monastery [K].   *reverend
room* place devoted to religious life.   26 *More than thou hast* different from
any residence you now have.   26 *joy* enjoy.   29 *High* noble.   31 *fear* object of
fear.   35 *of slander* that brings disgrace.

The guilt of conscience take thou for thy labour,
But neither my good word nor princely favour.
With Cain go wander thorough shades of night,
And never show thy head by day nor light.
Lords, I protest my soul is full of woe   45
That blood should sprinkle me to make me grow.
Come, mourn with me for what I do lament,
And put on sullen black incontinent.
I'll make a voyage to the Holy Land
To wash this blood off from my guilty hand.   50
March sadly after. Grace my mournings here
In weeping after this untimely bier.   *Exeunt.*

---

48 *sullen* gloomy, mournful. *incontinent* forthwith. 51 *Grace* do honour to.